THE INDIA RUBBER MAN

The Story of Billy Bly, Hull City's Longest-Serving Player

Roy Bly with David Bond

Published By

Tykesport Publications

2, Conifer Close,
Maplewood Avenue,
Hull,
East Yorkshire
HU5 5YU

£10

THE INDIA RUBBER MAN

CONTENTS

ACKNOWLEDGEMENTS

The authors are grateful for the help that has been afforded them by a number of people, including Billy Bly's family, friends and football colleagues, to bring this book to fruition.

The photographs in the book all come from Billy Bly's own private collection and scrapbooks. Some are family shots and most of the others do not have anything written on the back of them to give an indication of copyright. Where copyright is indicated and permission for use has not been given, then the photographs have been omitted. We have acknowledged copyright wherever possible, but it has been difficult to trace some organisations responsible for some of the older photographs. We are also grateful to the Grimsby Evening Telegraph for their permission to use some of their pictures, but we do sincerely apologise if any acknowledgement of the origin of any others has in ignorance been overlooked.

Typeset by D. J. Simmons
Origination by Marlin Studios Ltd., Hull
Printed by Allan Pipes Limited, Beverley

ISBN No. 0-9544015-0-6

THE INDIA RUBBER MAN

FOREWORD by the Rt. Hon. Sir Edward Heath, KG, MBE

Bill Bly was a renowned goalkeeper in English football from prewar days and he played a full and successful part in our regimental soccer after VE Day.

When I became second-in-command of the 86th Regiment of the Honourable Artillery Company in Germany in the autumn of 1945, I arranged to give a high priority to the creation of a regimental soccer team and we provided them with a good-sized ground, which was turned into a soccer pitch.

I then arranged for these members of the regiment to be excluded from guard duties and other commitments so that they could devote their whole time to soccer and to taking part in the football championship of the Rhine Army.

They all realised, of course, that, if they were beaten at any stage in the battle for the championship, they would lose their special accommodation and the soccer pitch!

The team proved to be a major attraction for the regiment and as many of their members as possible were taken by road to each match as spectators. The last match, which settled the whole affair, was held in Brussels and we were absolutely delighted with our regiment's victory. Our brigade became the proud possessors of the champion team in the British Army of the Rhine.

We were fortunate that we had sufficient top-class professionals permanently in the regiment to provide the winning team. Bill Bly played the leading part in it, not only through his own performance in goal, which was envied by every other team in the Rhine Army, but also because he was a tremendous inspiration to all our players.

I am indeed glad that Bill Bly's story is now to be published. Everyone will admire him.

Best Wishes

Bill Bly

A Life in Goal

It had never been Billy Bly's goal in life to spend a life in goal. Like so many young footballers before and after him, he started out as an outfield player and almost reluctantly and accidentally became a goalkeeper. In Billy's case, though, he turned out to be a special goalkeeper who spent most of his life as a professional footballer with one club, Hull City.

Nowadays footballers, aided and abetted by agents, tend to move from one club to another with alarming regularity, show scant regard for loyalty and simply aim to make as much money as they can in the shortest possible time. To a degree, it is understandable because a career in football can be brief, but it still creates moral dilemmas that were not so prevalent years ago. The days when players stayed with one club long enough to earn a testimonial after the traditional 10 years' service are largely long gone because money talks to the detriment of just about everything else. The era of the one-club men has largely evaporated.

But Billy Bly was one such player - and more. He was with Hull City, his only League club, for 23 years and it was only reluctantly that the club then offered him a testimonial game at the end of that time. He came from an age when players were effectively servants - possibly even slaves - to their clubs. It is ironic, therefore, that the maximum wage in football was abolished soon after Billy's League career had finally finished because players have bit by bit gained most of the power since then.

Billy Bly's life and times, therefore, emerged from a very different background from the football of the 21st century. He originated from Newcastle and made his first tentative steps towards soccer recognition when he was offered a trial with Hull City in 1937. He made the most of it and was in the Tigers' first team as an 18-year-old before his career was cut short by the Second World War almost as soon as it had started to blossom. Like most of his sporting contemporaries who lost some of the best years of their lives to the War, he had to make the best of the austerity, but he did underline his growing reputation as a goalkeeper when the opportunities arose.

The experience stood Billy in good stead when normal service was resumed and he went on to have a memorable League career with City that remarkably encompassed four decades. After his teenage baptism into League soccer in the 1930s, he established himself in what was left of the 1940s as his career and reputation prospered, helping the Tigers to promotion from the old Third Division North. During the 1950s there was a relegation and then a second promotion from the newly-established Third Division. But the optimism was short-lived and the 1960s heralded another relegation. It also signalled the end of Billy's long stay at Boothferry Park - a life within a life that was ended by the club in an unnecessarily caustic and callous fashion.

The fact that a loyal servant was treated badly led to a public outcry about the way in which the club handled Bly's departure from Boothferry Park. Billy himself was as diplomatic and dignified as ever about it, but it showed a major flaw in the club's make-up because they ditched their most durable employee ruthlessly and uncompromisingly. They gave the impression that they cared little for Billy the person: he was just a goalkeeping commodity who was suddenly of no further use to them. The statistics suggest otherwise.

Billy Bly played in 403 League games for City - from April 1937 to April 1960 - before his departure, which was communicated to him in the briefest, most remote way by the then manager, Bob Brocklebank, even though it simply reflected the harsh manner in which players were so often treated in those days. In that time the Tigers had played a total of 608 League matches - in the Second Division, the Third Division and the Third Division North. Bly had played in almost two-thirds of them, but the figures are undoubtedly misleading because the percentage would have been much higher if he had not repeatedly been held back by injuries, many of them serious.

During that same timespan the Tigers also played 48 postwar FA Cup ties and Bly was on duty for 37 of them, more than threequarters. Injuries meant that he missed five in a row between February 1950 and January 1953, so his record of missing only six in 12 other seasons stands up to the most rigorous scrutiny.

Bly also played in a number of other games for City, mainly friendlies, tour matches and East Riding Invitation Trophy ties. He appeared in two prewar benefit games against Scottish club Queen of the South - for Willie Savage and the Tigers' own Cliff Woodhead respectively - and then played in 35 out of 75 other matches in the postwar years. In this instance, though, the figure is deceptive. Quite often City gave opportunities to other goalkeepers on their books - most of them Bly's understudies - so his appearances were distinctly limited. It is cruelly ironic that he was selected for one friendly in 1954 - against another Scottish club, Falkirk - and was injured in it, depriving him of representative honours with England. But 10 other goalkeepers - Cyril Hannaby, Peter Atkinson, Joe Carter, Alec Corbett, Joe Robinson, Tommy Forgan, Dave Teece, Colin Gagen, Bernard Fisher and Barry Lord - all took their turns in varied postwar matches for City instead of Bly.

In addition, Bly occasionally played as a guest for other clubs during the difficult wartime years, but he still made a total of 18 appearances for the Tigers, the bulk of which were in the North Regional League during 1940-41. The others were in the North-East Regional League and the Football League Wartime Cup as organised soccer naturally became very fragmented.

It meant that Bly made a total of 493 first-team appearances for City at all levels and the 403 that he made in League football were significant. Bly remains fifth in the club's all-time appearances lists behind Andy Davidson, Garreth Roberts, George "Geordie" Maddison and Chris Chilton. And in 1960 he became only the second player in the club's history to reach the milestone of appearing in 400 League games. Curiously, the first player to have achieved the feat had been Maddison, who was also a goalkeeper, also from the North-East - Birtley in County Durham, in fact - and a mentor of Bly in his formative days with City when their respective careers briefly overlapped.

Billy Bly had become the only player to represent the club at first-team level during four different decades - the 1930s to the 1960s - and was days away from his 40th birthday when Hull City released him in those ignominious circumstances. It may well have been the case that his best days were behind him, but the club's cold, calculating attitude towards their longest servant did them little credit. The fans, with whom Bly had long had a special rapport, felt that he should have been given due recognition for his loyalty and that he should not be cast aside as just another statistic on soccer's scrap heap.

The effect that Billy Bly had on generations of football fans in East Yorkshire had been immense. The public respected him for his bravery and courage and his resilience to bounce back time and again from injury setbacks. It was a touch ironic that someone who worked devotedlly on his fitness should be handicapped by severe injuries on such a regular basis. But the fans knew that Billy gave everything single-mindedly and unswervingly to the cause and was prepared to defy the odds at all times, so it came as little surprise that in 1951 there was a report that said: "'Our India Rubber Man' is the affectionate description that Hull folks give to their daring goalkeeper, Billy Bly."

The sobriquet stuck. Colin Smith, in fact, was one of Billy's teammates who made sure that it did. A centre-forward who scored 26 goals in City's 1958-59 promotion campaign alongside him, Smith explained: "Billy's stretching exercises in training were unbelievable because he was so supple and I called him 'The India Rubber Man.'"

Smith was also one of a number of players who grew up watching Billy as a supporter and then found himself playing alongside him. It was possible, of course, only because Billy's time with the Tigers was so prodigious, but they were fans of his as fans and then as teammates. Their respect for Billy was duplicated from both outside and then inside the game and Smith added: "As kids growing up in Hull and having games of soccer, usually in the street, you pretended that you were either Billy Bly if you were in goal or Raich Carter if you were upfront. When I joined Hull City in 1956 after completing my National Service, the majority of the team whom I'd supported as a youngster had either retired or joined other clubs, but Billy Bly was one of the exceptions with my other heroes such as Tom Berry and Syd Gerrie. To think that I would be training with players whom I had waited hours to watch was mind-boggling."

Brian Bulless, a colleague of Bly for even longer, shared very similar thoughts as he grew up and represented Hull City Boys: "As a schoolboy footballer, it was my ambition to play for Hull City. I couldn't wait for Saturday afternoons to come so that I could go to Boothferry Park and watch the Tigers. Raich Carter was naturally everyone's favourite footballer. He was such a great player and a big influence with other players young and old. But in my opinion Billy Bly ran Raich a close second. Week in and week out his brilliant displays helped to make Hull City one of the most consistent teams in the Third Division North at the time."

Another teammate, Mike Brown, who went on to become Manchester United's chief scout by the 21st century, took up the theme when he said: "When I was a kid, Billy was the man and he was one of my heroes. He had a big influence and was like a folk hero to me."

At the same time it is decidedly curious to contemplate the fact of football life that in recent times Billy would probably have never even had the opportunity to make the grade as a goalkeeper at all because the trend is firmly towards a different physical type. Billy was not big and his height was variously given as about 5ft. 9in. or 5ft. 10in. with the odd fraction thrown in here and there. At one stage he was 5ft.9¼in. and at another point he had grown to 5ft.10½in. Whatever figure might have been definitive, the stark fact of life is that it would still have counted against him nowadays. After all, the modern goalkeeper is normally expected to be something of a man mountain - more than 6ft. tall with an impressive build and an imposing physical presence that suggests that he fills the goal impressively. Smaller goalkeepers are now deemed to be something of risk against the rough and tumble of the game and there is less scope for them to make progress. When Billy played, though, there was far more acceptance of a slightly-built goalkeeper with a slim, lithe frame. More of them abounded then provided that they were agile, decisive, positive and courageous. Billy was, so he was given the opportunity to flourish.

The whole concept, though, is something of a paradox. When the smaller goalkeepers such as Billy were around, they were buffeted with monotonous regularity by opponents. They had to be prepared to endure something known as a fair shoulder charge from opposing forwards and they would probably have laughed at the suggestion that one day it would be outlawed. Years ago goalkeepers were expected to accept it as part and parcel of the game and expected to withstand it. A look at consecutive FA Cup finals of the 1950s reinforces the theory. Bert Trautmann became a hero with Manchester City in 1956 when he played on with a broken neck in a collision with Peter Murphy against Birmingham City and then there was the physical bombardment inflicted on consecutive Manchester United goalkeepers Ray Wood and Harry Gregg in 1957 and 1958 respectively. All the instances took place - as did the whole of Billy Bly's playing career - in the pre-substitute days. Nowadays, though, bigger goalkeepers proliferate and yet they are something of a protected species. Physical assaults by opposing forwards are punished by referees quickly and effectively and goalkeepers - even though they are largely larger - have become the untouchables.

Charlie Crickmore, a winger who played alongside Billy in the later stages of his career at Boothferry Park, took up the point. Crickmore, who had a spell as a referee after his playing days had ended, reflected: "Although Billy wasn't tall, he was very agile and brave. He would regularly come out and shut people down and smother things, but in those days forwards would just go through the goalkeepers. Nowadays they'd get at least a yellow card if it happened, but, when we played, they'd go through the goalkeepers five or six times before the referees would even think about booking them."

Billy came from a generation of goalkeepers who knew that they had to have the resolve to tolerate assault and battery on the football field - or else. It was very surprising, therefore, that some of them survived at all. It is entirely bewildering that some of them, such as Billy, enjoyed lengthy careers. Goalkeepers generally are reckoned to have longer shelf lives in the game than outfield players, but it goes against the grain when it is remembered that years ago they always had to put up with such extreme physical offensives.

Billy Bly, though, appeared to be unbeatable by time as well as by opposing forwards. He left League football with Hull City shortly before his 40th birthday, but amazingly his links with the FA Cup were not over. In the autumn of 1961 in the autumn of his goalkeeping career he dramatically responded to the call to arms to bale out non-League Weymouth in an emergency. It brought him three more FA Cup appearances and a brief flirtation with Southern League football.

Even then his playing career continued a while longer in local non-League football in East Yorkshire with Brunswick Institute, later Hull Brunswick. He also worked assiduously behind the scenes with Brunswick during the 1960s and North Ferriby United in the 1970s. The outcome was that in 1985 - three years after his death - his name was preserved in local football lore with an annual match between Hull City and North Ferriby for the Billy Bly Memorial Trophy, which still exists, traditionally as a pre-season fixture.

Billy was also a devoted family man and had other interests and skills, such as gardening, drawing and cobbling. And while he will always be remembered in the public domain as a footballer and, more specifically, as a goalkeeper, he enjoyed other sports - at an arm's length.

His son, Roy, said: "Dad was generally interested in other sports, but only at a distance. He did like bowls and used to play occasionally with one of his City teammates, Ernie Phillips, and thoroughly enjoyed it. He also loved to watch athletics and encouraged my sister, Norma, when she was younger. And he was pally with some of the local rugby-league players, such as the Drakes and the Whiteleys."

At one stage Billy even turned his goalkeeping hands to Continental handball and Roy added: "Dad had massive hands with a big spread, so the handball was easy meat for him because it was smaller than a football. He played at Costello Park in Hull and enjoyed it because it was a way of relaxing to him." The sport combined elements of soccer, rugby, netball and basketball and plans to form a Continental handball league between April and November were formulated at a meeting at the Burns Head Hotel in Hull's Charles Street in March 1958.

Hull City's two experienced goalkeepers, Billy Bly and Bernard Fisher, took part as the sport developed although they would doubtless have been banned from doing so nowadays. And Fisher, the City goalkeeper who worked most closely with Billy during his later years at Boothferry Park, remembered: "The game was played with 11 players on a full-sized pitch, just like for soccer. But hands were used a bit like basketball although goalposts were used for scoring. Billy played for a team called Asbestos, I played for Hull Boys' Club and several local rugby-league players, such as John Whiteley and Sam Evans, took part. Eight teams formed the league and Asbestos won it. To the best of my knowledge, the game was played only in Hull, but a match was arranged between England and Germany with Billy in goal."

It might well have been some small compensation for the lack of recognition for Billy's goalkeeping ability at international level. Ill-luck had robbed him of his chance of playing for England B in the spring of 1954 when he received one of his many injuries after having been called up. The injury came in a meaningless friendly arranged by the Tigers against Falkirk at Boothferry Park and the club made it worse when they unsuccessfully tried to rob him of some pay because he was unable to complete the game!

In some ways, in fact, it is perhaps a touch bewildering that Billy stuck it out for so long with City because there is little doubt that he could have moved on to a bigger club on several occasions. He attracted top-flight interest from his early postwar days and received praise and plaudits when he was at his peak after he had established himself as a high-quality goalkeeper for his part in the Tigers' promotion from the Third Division North as champions in 1948-49.

One good reason why he probably never played in what was then First Division soccer was the part played in his development by the War years. So many sportsmen lost some of their best years to the conflict and Billy was no exception. After all, he made his first League appearance for the Tigers as an 18-year-old and stayed in the side for eight matches. But he did not play his ninth League game for the club until he was 26 - at the opening of Boothferry Park. The War had robbed him of some of the best footballing years of his life and it is in that context that his future in the game had then always to be put.

He was 29 shortly after the Tigers had won promotion and he was looking forward to a taste of Second Division football for the first time. He was in his prime, but perhaps he was deemed to have a comparatively short career left by then. Maybe that was unfair to him because goalkeepers are known for their soccer longevity and he was, after all, nearly 34 when he received that aborted call-up to the England B squad. In fact, Manchester United's tragic hero Duncan Edwards, one of the victims of the Munich Air Disaster, was also in the party at the age of 17!

Whether Billy should have earned himself a move or not, he defied age as much as he defied onrushing opponents because he celebrated a second promotion with the Tigers when he was only a few weeks short of his 39th birthday. He had demonstrated loyalty to his club in an era when it was part and parcel of life rather than the apparent afterthought that it so often seems to be nowadays. To all intents and purposes footballers were soccer slaves during Billy Bly's League career. It may have lasted a long time, but it was still in the days before concepts such as the abolition of the maximum wage, freedom of contract and the Bosman ruling took effect to make such a vast difference to players' wages.

It may have been ironic that the maximum wage was indeed invalidated soon after he had been released by Hull City. But the remnants of the Corinthian approach remained during Billy Bly's day and players did not openly rebel at the drop of the first wage packet. They played more for love than money and their contracts were far more akin to the earnings of the average man in the street. Football may have been their business, but it was also their pleasure and Billy's philosophical and dedicated attitude reflected it.

2

Geordie Boy

Billy Bly was born into a large family at 150 Church Street in the Walker area of Newcastle on May 15, 1920, in the registration district of Tynemouth. He was the son of William Hicks-Bly, a shipwright, and Annie Bly, formerly Forrest, who had had seven other children before him. Billy's father, in fact, had also come from a large family because he was the eldest of 11 children, most of whom lived in different houses along Church Street although one sister, Grace, lived in George Street and one brother, George, lived in New Road. The line can be further traced to Tom Bly, a plater by trade, and his wife, Jane, to Joseph Hicks, a shipwright and beer retailer, and to William Hicks, who died in May 1863 at the age of 60, before him.

Billy Bly's father, William, kept things simple and his grandson, Roy, explained: "It was a double-barrelled name, but he always used just Bly. He was part of a well-to-do family and a large household, but my grandma had been a maid or a servant and had got together with the owner's son. But the family didn't like it."

Billy Bly had two brothers, Ernest and Roy, but for different reasons he was always closer to his five sisters - Maud, Lily, Winnie, Hilda and Annie. Ernest, the eldest of the eight, went to live with another section of the family while he was brought up, while Roy tragically lived only a few days. Billy's son, Roy, who was named after his uncle, said: "I remember going to 150 Church Street in Walker, which is by the side of Walker Park playing-fields. There was a shop and the family occupied the top flat. Inside it was a living-room, a kitchen and one bedroom, but all those people had to live there, so my uncle Ernest was farmed out to a relative in Northumberland and grew up separately. But it wasn't uncommon in those days because at the time there were big families around. I never met my uncle Ernest, but everyone seemed to have big families and it wasn't unheard-of for the older ones to be moved out and to lose touch with them."

Equally, Billy's five sisters moved around and none of them stayed long in the North-East once they had grown up. Maud married Billy Mawson, a Yorkshire Dalesman who became the gardener at Hughenden Manor, near High Wycombe. They also lived in West Wycombe and, according to Roy: "It used to be Benjamin Disraeli's house and became a National Trust property when they bought it from the Rowntree's chocolates family in the 1950s. It is a museum nowadays, but dad often took us down there on holiday." Lily and her husband, George Cluckson, moved to Dalkeith, near Edinburgh, while Winnie also lived in Buckinghamshire eventually. But she and her husband, Bob Howitt, originally lived on Tyneside at Cullercoats, near Whitley Bay. Roy recalled: "Bob was a railwayman and he used to get free travel to take me to St. James' Park to watch Newcastle United when I visited them as a boy. But later they moved south to Amersham, where Bob was the caretaker at the local council offices." Hilda and Annie, meanwhile, moved even further south with their families and lived in the Parkstone area of Dorset. Hilda and her husband, Tom Astley, initially stayed in Newcastle, but Roy said: "We used to stay with Annie and her husband, Bert Gubbins, for family holidays and my dad stayed with her when he played for Weymouth towards the end of his football career."

Billy's cousin, Jim, who was born in 1931 and lives in Whitley Bay, remembers the prewar days in Walker as he grew up in the 1930s. He cannot remember meeting Billy, who had been born 11 years earlier, but he recalled: "A lot of the family lived in Church Street, which was a very long road, and Billy Bly's house was on the west side. My Aunt Annie lived almost opposite it and was married to a small, but very vocal chap called Tommy Farrell. He was either Irish or of Irish stock and we all liked him. We lived on the same side as the Farrells - firstly at No. 205 and then at No. 221, so we were all only a few hundred yards away from each other. It is surprising then that we didn't live in each other's pockets although we visited the Farrells fairly often. I can remember being in Billy's father's house only once and I must have been about three or four at the time. But I certainly knew Billy's father, William, and his wife, Annie, who was, by all accounts, a nice woman.

"I have no remembrance of seeing Billy, but I did know of him and I wrote to him in Hull when I was in my teens. He was kind enough to let me have copies of his autograph for my schoolmates. We always remembered him as having injuries while he was playing football. In fact, I think he was well-known for them. And I do know that my father, Jim, always referred to him with some pride as 'Wor Billy's son.'"

The young Billy Bly, in fact, was soon interested in soccer, as befits someone from the North-East, an area for so long renowned as one of its hotbeds. He kept records of teams and their appearances, one example being when he diligently wrote down the names, heights and weights of the Newcastle United players of the early 1930s. Interestingly, one name on his list was Sam Weaver, the long-throw expert who had joined the Magpies from Hull City.

But Roy recalled: "No-one had much money and home was a rented, three-roomed flat above a sweet shop. The cobbled back way at home was often the place for my dad to have a game of soccer with his mates. And his home was near to the main gates of Walker Park, where, as a boy, he played for endless hours with a ball made out of rolled paper and tied up with string."

As a schoolboy, Billy used to go to St. James' Park to watch Newcastle United, where he paid special attention to their goalkeeper, Albert McInroy, who had briefly played for England during his first spell with Sunderland. And Billy later admitted in an interview: "I suppose that I wished, like lots of other lads, that I could catch a ball as he did."

At that time Billy was already playing as a goalkeeper for his school, West Walker, but he said: "I didn't stay in goal for very long because I decided that it was too cold a job for me." Accordingly, he then became a full-back before switching to centre-half at Welbeck Road School and earning a call-up for Newcastle Boys as a left-half.

In April 1933 Billy was chosen by Newcastle Schools' association football section as a reserve for the Infirmary Cup game between Newcastle Boys and Chester-le-Street Boys at Raby United's ground. The postcard informing him of his selection instructed him: "Bring boots and a towel." And it added a rider that was a touch ironic in view of his injury record as a professional footballer in later years: "If the boy is unable to play or if there is any doubt as to his fitness, please write at once to Mr. E. Nendick, 223 Tamworth Road, Newcastle."

Five months later the association football representative at Welbeck Upper School received further correspondence about Billy, who was by then 13. Again it was from the Newcastle Schools' association football section, who indicated that Billy had been chosen for what they called their town team trials. He was told to report to Forsyth Road playing-field on Wednesday, September 27, at 4.30pm. The other details included: "Boys are to report to Mr. Nendick and should bring a towel each. Jerseys only will be supplied - goalkeepers to supply own."

There was another reason why Billy did not relish the prospect of goalkeeping. Roy explained: "He played as a half-back for Welbeck Road School, but the teacher kept putting him into goal and he didn't like it because he wasn't big. He was light and he was thin and a few years later he had to stop playing because of problems with his ankles."

But it was just as if fate were dictating that he would be a goalkeeper whatever the circumstances, so Billy finally went along with it. But he remained reluctant and reticent about the prospects and he reflected: "When I look back on my early days, I sometimes wonder why I became a goalkeeper at all. I hated the position at school after being Press-ganged to make up the side by one of my teachers. It was too cold for me and I wanted to be running about like the other lads. Eventually I won trials for Newcastle Boys as a left-half, but I was advised to give up playing when I left school because I had weak ankles. My teacher advised father that a lay-off would be wise to allow my ankles to get a bit stronger and, although it was very tempting when I saw my pals kicking a ball about, I stuck it out for 12 months."

Billy then had a season with Walker Boys' Club, playing mainly as a left-winger and occasionally as a centre-forward, but still he was haunted by the expectation that he was meant to be a goalkeeper. He explained: "When 'our gang' decided to start a youth club and a soccer team were formed, they tried to work me into goal again. I wasn't having any of it this time and finally settled for a spot in the forward-line until our goalkeeper was hurt and I was pretty well forced to take over - only after a solemn promise that I would have my forward place back when he recovered. But just before the end of the season I went into goal once more and there I've been ever since."

He then had a brief spell with a more senior club called Walker Temperance, but left them after they had basically told him that he was no good! Billy said: "I was invited to fill the vacancy when they found themselves a goalkeeper short. But the committee decided that I was not big enough after a couple of games, so it was back to the youth club."

Almost immediately, though, Billy signed for Walker Celtic, his local club in the North Eastern League, playing his first game in the reserves in February 1937 and earning promotion to the first team a month later. He recalled: "I had decided to give up fighting fate and to make myself as good a goalkeeper as possible, so I got my rewards when Walker Celtic picked me up. But I was only 16 and weighed 8st. 12lb., so some said that I was too young and others that I was too small. We were beaten 6-0 in that first game, but I saved a penalty and kept my place in the team to the end of the season."

Much as he was starting to love his football, Billy had at the same time to contemplate the serious business of finding a career after leaving school. He lived in Wallsend and he began to learn his trade as a painter and decorator. Football was a hobby and there was no suggestion at that stage that it would provide him with a career outlet.

Roy said: "After leaving school, dad went into an apprenticeship for painting and decorating. He had still been progressing with his art, but it was not an economical option or high on his father's list of priorities. As a result, he often cycled miles to learn his trade and used to go round on his bicycle from one job to another, meeting the guy who was training him. I think he spent nearly three years serving his time. He was nearly pushed into working in the shipyard, which was just down at the bottom of the road. And he did work for a few months as a painter on the ships on the River Tyne, where my granddad and his brother, whom I never met, used to work."

But Walker Celtic were a nursery team for Newcastle United and Billy's performances in goal for them began to attract attention from League clubs. And the possibility of Billy becoming a professional footballer did not seem so far-fetched, after all.

In an ideal world, though, Billy might also have turned his artistic ability to good use and not have had to embark on his apprenticeship as a painter and decorator. Roy said: "One thing that my father had to decide was whether to follow football for a career or develop his artistic skills, but you needed money in those days to develop your art. The family couldn't afford to keep him while he was progressing in art and in the end it became his hobby. But he had a passion and a talent for art and often sketched cartoons. Curiously, the characters would regularly be professional footballers. He was marvellous at sketching and drawing and he really should have put more time into it because he was so gifted. Instead he would draw cartoons or sketch little things round the house.

"I still have an old rice-paper book and it contains charcoal-crayoned illustrations of still life that he produced in his early days. Some of them look as if they are a child's efforts, but others have so much detail. The schoolbooks show what a talent he had and in one of his art books from 1933 the teachers' marks show eight out of 10 and nine out of 10 with merits. They are still-life colour drawings of a postbox, a book, a banana and orange and an Army helmet. They are full of details and are of outstanding appearance considering that my dad was only 13 then."

But if Billy had been unsure about his future, then there was also a question-mark about Walker Celtic's prospects when he played for them as a 16-year-old. Their future was causing concern in the mid-1930s despite their reputation because it was reported: "Walker Celtic have carried themselves to safety. It must have been a Herculean struggle at the Alkan Ground, but there is little doubt about their ability to carry on. There is a such a wealth of talent in the small clubs in their area and the lads seem to regard Celtic as a stepping-stone to better-class soccer. Bly, their brilliant, young goalkeeper, is a typical example. Six weeks ago he was in junior football. Now several big clubs fancy he would be worth nursing for a couple of seasons."

The Tigers were to be at the forefront of the queue for him and he subsequently did manage to fit in two seasons with them before the Second World War. The prediction, though, turned out to have erred a little on the cautious side because it did not take into account the further 14 seasons that Billy was to spend at Boothferry Park after the War...

3

The Road to Hull

Hull City had already earned themselves a reputation for acquiring goalkeepers from the North-East by the time that they offered a trial to Billy Bly. The line had started in their first season in the League when Martin Spendiff, from North Shields, was an ever-present in the Second Division in 1905-06. Soon afterwards Ernest Storey, who was from Birtley in County Durham, appeared briefly in the first team, while Nicolson Hendry, who had been with Middlesbrough as an amateur and then Darlington even though he was originally from York, also established himself before the First World War. In the early 1920s Arthur Briggs had the occasional run-out in the Tigers' first team and he, in fact, set a trend because, just like Bly, he had been born in Newcastle and had played for Walker Celtic. Then came the long-serving George "Geordie" Maddison, who joined City in the summer of 1924 and was also from Birtley.

Maddison was still at Anlaby Road when Billy Bly ventured south to try his luck in 1937, but he was coming to the end of his career and his recognised deputy, Eddie Goodall, was also from the North-East. Goodall, who played more first-team games than Maddison in Bly's first season with the Tigers, was born in South Shields and had played for Jarrow and North Shields. But both Maddison and Goodall had left City by the time that the 1938-39 season arrived and John Ellis, who had been signed from Bristol Rovers, was designated as the new first-choice goalkeeper. Ellis followed in City's line of Lancastrian goalkeepers such as Ed Roughley and Billy Mercer, but his senior deputy was Ben Darling, who was signed from his home-town club, South Shields, in the summer of 1938 and was four years older than Bly.

The plans for Billy Bly to join Hull City were formulated during the summer of 1937 after a scout in the North-East had recommended him to the club. The initial idea was for the 17-year-old goalkeeper to join City for a month on trial during their build-up to the 1937-38 season, but Billy admitted: "I wasn't keen on the idea, but I agreed to arrange my holidays so that I could travel to Hull for a trial game." The Tigers' manager, Ernie Blackburn, accordingly wrote to Billy's father, William, to inform him of their plans on July 21, 1937.

Blackburn's letter read: "Our Mr. Robson, of Gateshead, has written to me and also forwarded on to us the form signed by your son for our club. I am very grateful that you have allowed him to do this. Now I understand that Mr. Robson has promised that you can come down and bring the lad for a week on trial in August. At the moment the dates for our practices have not been fixed, but I expect that the week from August 14 to 21 will be when I should like you down with him. Can you make this convenient? Please let me know and, if necessary otherwise, I will try to arrange accordingly.

"We will, of course, pay your expenses, and I hope you will have a happy time. I feel sure that you will find us very amiable and you need have no fear about your son because I will do what I can to help him. In the meantime, while you are here, we may be able to do something, if necessary, as to his apprenticeship with some painter or other here in Hull. However, I have not had much time to deal with this matter. Therefore, you must excuse me for the present. I will go into it and see what can be done.

"Will you let me know if the week mentioned - August 14 to 21, Saturday to Saturday - would suit you? Thanking you once again and wishing the boy every success and yourself the best of wishes."

The headed club notepaper confirmed that Blackburn was both City's manager and secretary - they also had a financial secretary, though - so he acted efficiently and regularly by letter. William Bly responded immediately and on July 23 Blackburn replied to him with a note of caution because the plans could not be finalised until negotiations with Hull Cricket Club had taken place.

Blackburn's letter read this time: "Please do not make any definite arrangements for any dates yet to come down here because we are having difficulty in arranging dates for our practices with the cricket club, who are the owners of our ground and whose permission we have to get to play matches on it during the period prior to the football season's League matches commencing. We may get permission for only one Saturday match because of clashing with their cricket fixtures. You see we have to pass through the cricket ground to get to our football ground, just like the Darlington club grounds.

"If we can play only one game on a Saturday - I presume a weekend would suffice for you and the boy to come along - we could then discuss matters affecting the boy's future career and you would see us all here. It may also be more convenient for you from the point of view of getting away from your work for a day or two than a whole week. However, I will write to you again as soon as definite arrangements for our matches are made. Thanking you once again."

Almost a fortnight later Blackburn confirmed further details of the Tigers' plans for the trial in the context of their pre-season build-up when he wrote to William Bly on August 4: "We have now fixed the dates for our trial matches. They are on Thursday, August 12, for local amateurs, Monday, August 16, and Saturday, August 21. The kick-off each day is at 6.45pm and the last two are for professionals.

"Do you think that Monday, August 16, would suit the boy? What about coming down with him? Will you be coming or will you let him come by himself? Please let me know what you think best. We will see that he is all right in every respect.

"Up to now I have had no luck in getting him fixed up with his trade. Anyhow we can discuss matters with you later on and then anything you wish to mention can be gone into regarding his future. I shall be pleased to hear from you as to the best date suitable."

Two days later William Bly wrote back to Blackburn to let him know of the preferences as everything proceeded in a very businesslike way. It was ironically in direct contrast with the way in which the club were to dispense with Billy's services many years later and Blackburn, in turn, confirmed the basic arrangements with another letter to his father on August 11.

It read: "I note that August 16 is convenient for you and the boy. Therefore, will you bring the lad down on Monday next and he can then play in a trial match that night? I will give you a list of trains from Newcastle to Hull.

"We will, of course, pay your out-of-pocket expenses and, because it will be necessary for you to stay overnight, we can arrange for this. We will also pay your fares, which will amount to 21 shillings each. Shall I forward you the cash to book or can you manage until you come down here?

"Please let me know by return so that I can arrange the teams, etc., accordingly. If you cannot come down that day, then I shall have to leave it until matches commence.

"We can have a talk as to the boy's future, etc., on your arrival. Hoping to see you on

Monday next and I hope the boy will do well. Please let me know about coming."

The tones of Blackburn's letters suggested that City were in principle interested in signing Billy provided that he came through the trial satisfactorily. The fact that Blackburn referred considerably to looking after Billy's future in general hinted that the club were prepared to do their utmost to help him if he proved to be a worthwhile investment as a goalkeeper.

As it turned out, William Bly did not accompany his son on the trial trip because Roy Bly said: "Letters were exchanged and the arrangements were eventually made to go down to Hull on trial on the train. My grandfather was invited, but in the end he sent my dad down on his own, which was quite a big step for a young fellow."

At the same time Billy was very close to missing his big chance to impress because it was touch and go as to whether he arrived in time for the public practice match. He thought that there had either been a misunderstanding about the kick-off time or his train was late because it was nearly halftime when he arrived at Anlaby Road. He later reflected: "There was just time for me to strip and be ready to take George Maddison's place in the second half. George said: 'Don't be scared! Just think that you're playing with the boys at home!'"

As it was, the trial went well and Billy the Kid was immediately taken on to the staff for the 1937-38 season. In fact, it all happened very quickly because Blackburn signed him only an hour after the trial on August 16 itself and a week later Billy set off back to Hull to start his career in professional football.

He was unperturbed about having to move away and uproot from Tyneside to East Yorkshire while still only a teenager. Billy put the prospects pertinently into perspective and Roy said: "My dad knew of the Jarrow March and he knew how hard it was in the North-East because he'd had a taste of the shipyards and the docks and he wanted a better life. Many of his family and friends were in the shipyards and I think he asked himself if he really wanted to be there, too. He came down to Hull on trial and did well. And I think he wanted to make a professional goalkeeper because football would bring stability."

Harold Meens, who was to become a teammate and one of his closest friends, was at the station to meet him on his return to Yorkshire. Billy had agreed to a contract, lasting until May 7, 1938, that offered him £2. 10s. per week and the official witness to it was his father, William. His address was given as 150 Church Street, Walker-on-Tyne.

The contracts of the day had nine clauses, some of which were phrased intriguingly. One read: "The player hereby agrees to play in an efficient manner and to the best of his ability for the club." Another insisted: "The player shall not engage in any business or live in any place which the directors or the committee of the club may deem unsuitable."

Bly was also issued with a player's ticket for the season and it makes interesting reading, too. It indicated, for example, a guideline to the season's kick-off times, which varied in those pre-floodlight days from 3.15pm at the start and the end to 2.15pm in December. The club also issued players with 13 bye-laws and training rules, which included an instruction to report for training twice daily - at 10am and 2.30pm - as requested. Match jerseys were not to be used for training purposes and players were not to visit the club's medical officer without first obtaining permission to do so. Players were to report for a home game only 45 minutes before the kick-off and they were given a warning about bad language on and off the field because it "lowers the dignity of the individual and the prestige of the team." And there were off-the-field rules such as: "Players must not ride motor-cycles at any time. Any player injured in such a way will forfeit all claims of wages from the club." Other pastimes were discouraged: "Smoking is prohibited in the dressing-rooms and gambling of any description will not be permitted on the club premises. Players are also to note that certain games of cards are forbidden when travelling to and from away matches." Socialising was also restricted: "Players must not enter premises licensed for the sale of intoxicating drink after Monday in each week nor attend any dance after Tuesday in each week unless in the charge of a responsible official of the club or with permission from the manager or the trainer. Players must be in their places of residence by 10.45 on the night before a match unless in the charge of a responsible official of the club."

It was against such a backcloth that Billy Bly, who moved into 14 Perry Street, Hull., all of a sudden found himself preparing for life as a professional footballer alongside two other goalkeepers from the North-East, Maddison and Goodall. But Billy recalled: "I was so frail at the time - 8st. 12lb. - that I got only occasional reserve-team games for the first 18 months at Hull as I underwent a body-building course."

Maddison had long been acknowledged as the club's first-choice goalkeeper and he played in 14 out of the first 15 League games in 1937-38, but he was 35 a fortnight before the start of the season and was having injury problems. He made only two more first-team appearances for the club and his retirement was on the cards. The last home fixture of the season - at home to Crewe Alexandra - was designated as Maddison's benefit match, but he had still made his mark on the young Billy Bly in the one season that they had together at Anlaby Road.

Maddison did his best to encourage and nurture Billy's talent and readily passed on his advice and experience. Roy Bly recalled: "I can remember my father telling me that 'Geordie' Maddison treated him like a son, but he ruled with an iron fist. My father wouldn't move without his permission. 'Geordie' really had a hold on him, but for all the right reasons, such as the discipline.

"My dad once told me that they were on a coach and he was part of the squad with 'Geordie' Maddison, who had been looking after him. They stopped and were getting off the coach to go and have a drink. But 'Geordie' turned round to my dad and said: 'You're not coming because you're not allowed to. There's no alcohol for you.' So my dad had to stay on the coach. But, funnily enough, I can honestly say that I never saw my father drink pints of beer in my company - even at home.

"My father used to say that Maddison was one of the most experienced goalkeepers around. He was a strict disciplinarian and my dad took a lot of advice from him, which benefited his career. Everybody who saw my father play could see his natural talent, but he'd still got to work hard at some of it. He told me that 'Geordie' helped with the technical side of it when he tied ropes round the goalposts to teach him the angles. My dad never went into any details about it, so I don't know in what manner he did it, but I believe that the ropes were all laid at different angles so that he had an idea where his six-yard box and the penalty spot were. The idea was that you'd got a split second to make decisions, so you'd to got to think of the angles and where you were."

Billy himself was full of gratitude for Maddison's counsel because he said: "My first job was to put on some weight. I didn't get a lot of chances in those early days, but I was learning all the time. I was just a goal-line 'keeper when I came to Hull, but George Maddison used to take me out and demonstrate how to narrow angles and he gave me all sorts of useful tips."

Maddison, in fact, kept a close watch on his protégé from a distance for a long time after his own playing career had ended. And years later Billy confessed: "George still tells me very plainly what he thinks about my Saturday-afternoon efforts because he lives not far away and rarely misses a home game."

Maddison, in fact, left City at the end of the 1937-38 season, but the similarities between him and Bly, who was to emerge as his natural successor, were striking. Both were originally from the North-East, both were to suffer serious injuries in pursuit of their goalkeeping craft - Maddison's setbacks had included two broken collarbones and a broken wrist - and they were the first two Hull City players to appear in more than 400 League games for the club. Maddison called it a day with 430 to his credit: Bly, on the other hand, had first to establish himself in the first team. He was still learning his trade and Blackburn brought in two new goalkeepers in the summer of 1938, Ellis and Darling, to compensate for Maddison's retirement and Goodall's move to Bolton Wanderers.

At the same time there was no doubt that City would keep Bly on after his first season with the club and Blackburn quickly offered him a further year's contract. Curiously, it was signed on May 6, 1938 - the day before Maddison's benefit match - and there were some amendments to it. In fact, it added up to a loss of income. Quite simply, Billy had been paid his £2. 10s. a week throughout the first year, but now there was an adjustment in the club's favour because he was offered less during the close season. He remained on £2. 10s. from August 1, 1938, to May 6, 1939, but he was now to receive only £1. 10s. from May to August in 1938. This time the contract was witnessed by surgeon Thomas Hardie, of 258 Anlaby Road, Hull. But there had been a clause in both contracts of which Billy, then of 14 Perry Street, Hull, was to take full advantage. It offered him "£1 extra per week when playing in the first team."

Blackburn had kept in touch with Billy during the summer and wrote to him on July 4, 1938, asking him to acknowledge the plans for the 1938-39 season: "Just a line to let you know that you must report for training on Tuesday, August 2. I suppose you have fixed up for your lodgings. Best wishes and I hope you are quite well."

City had been pipped for promotion from the Third Division North in 1937-38 when they lost their penultimate game of the season to the eventual champions, Tranmere Rovers. They ultimately finished third and did not do as well in 1938-39. For example, they lost 6-1 away to New Brighton and 6-2 away to Bradford City in their final two games of 1938 and then beat Carlisle United 11-1 - still their record victory - in the first game of 1939. Ellis played in most of the games and Darling had appeared just twice in the League and once in the FA Cup, but he received a head injury that gave Bly the opportunity to play for the reserves in the Midland League. By the end of March, though, it was time for Bly to progress even further because City were well out of the promotion race.

It meant that on April 1, 1939, the 18-year-old Billy Bly was given his League debut in the Tigers' game away to Rotherham United. It was reported: "Startling changes are made by Hull City on Saturday. Ellis, the goalkeeper secured from Bristol Rovers in the close season, is left out and Bly, a lad from Tyneside who has shown consistent form with the reserves this season, is introduced for the first time. " Ellis had, in fact, played his last senior game for the club - a 3-3 draw at home to Rochdale - and Bly had been offered the chance of playing what was to be his first of many.

Centre-half Harold Meens, who was a few months older than Bly and had made his own League debut for the Tigers in February 1939, had predicted it. Billy remembered: "Harold Meens prepared me for it the previous Saturday when he got back to our lodgings. He told me: 'You'll be in the first team next week.' I laughed at him, but I knew there was a chance when they put me on the scales on the Wednesday and sure enough my name was there to play against Rotherham United at Millmoor."

Billy recalled that he weighed 9st. 13lb. at the time and his call-up was proof that it had finally been accepted that he had the build to cope with first-team football. He had needed to show from the outset of his career that he had the physique to deal with the rigours of League soccer and even a postwar pen picture portrayed Billy's initial predicament as he honed his skills under Maddison's tutelage bit by bit: "As a boy in Newcastle, he showed more than average ability, but he failed to develop physically and still weighed less than eight stones at the age of 16. Some said that he was too frail ever to make a good goalkeeper, but he persisted and gradually put on weight."

At any rate Bly attained every goalkeeper's dream in every game - a clean sheet - on his debut at Millmoor because City won 2-0 with goals in each half by George Richardson. The second did not come until the closing stages and the Tigers were put under pressure in the second half as mid-table Rotherham sought an equaliser, but Bly acquitted himself well. In fact, it was sufficient for him to feature in a headline straightaway: "Bly impresses with good display in Tigers' goal." It was also reported: "Bly was as cool as a cucumber." He had made his mark immediately.

Bly did enough to keep his first-team place in the remaining seven games although City's form continued to be patchy and he twice let in four goals - at Southport and Oldham. They won three, drew two and lost three in Bly's eight appearances and finished seventh in the table. But 10 days after making his debut he agreed a new contract with City and, with just four League games under his belt, he was awarded a pay rise. This time the club's trainer Joe Beck, who lived at 131 Walton Street, Hull, witnessed the signing as Bly accepted £3 a week from July 29, 1939, to May 4, 1940. And now that he had tasted League soccer, he doubtless relished the prospect of being given more opportunities - he was still on the £1 bonus for being in the first team - but nothing is ever as simple as it ought to be.

For a start, Blackburn signed a new goalkeeper, Jack Curnow, in May 1939. He was originally from North Yorkshire, but had been in the Tranmere side who had been Third Division North champions in 1937-38, dramatically ruining City's promotion chances towards the end of the season. Ellis moved on to Clapton Orient and Darling was released during the summer, but Curnow was the Tigers' first-choice goalkeeper at the start of the 1939-40 campaign.

Curnow played in City's first two games in the Third Division North, but, of course, things were about to change much more dramatically almost immediately after the second one on September 2. A second World War broke out, competitive football was abandoned and it was to be a long time before Billy Bly got any further chance to play for Hull City's first team again in the accepted structure of League soccer.

4

International Duty

Billy Bly was one of those youngsters who was unlucky enough to have been born at the wrong time because he lost some of the best years of his sporting career to the 1939-45 War. In his case he had had his first taste of League soccer, but a world war had broken out before he could establish himself as a first-team regular with Hull City. He had broken into their first team while still only a teenager, but any sense of continuity was disrupted by the world crisis.

It was frustrating for an up-and-coming footballer, but the hiatus caused by the conflict was not something that people thought too much about. Football had been one job and now there was a very different one to do. One had been plenteously pleasant and the other was potently unpleasant. No-one could have forecast the length of the strife and its ramifications. The tiros who were plunged into the forefront of a world crisis were doing their bit for their country and it probably never dawned on them them how long it would last. The seven years' warfare, though, took a large portion out of a lot of young lives and those who were in Billy Bly's age bracket suffered more than most - if they were lucky enough to return home safely in the first instance, of course.

It all meant that the 1939-40 football season was over almost before it started in England because of the hostilities. City drew games against Lincoln City and Southport in the Third Division North before the whole programme was terminated and Jack Curnow was in goal for them. There then followed 22 fixtures in the North-East Regional League and five games in the Football League War Cup. They stretched from October 1939 to June 1940 and Curnow played in all but one of them. Bly, in the meantime, had returned to his native Tyneside to work in the local shipyard although he played in the other fixture - a 3-2 defeat at Hartlepools United on February 24, 1940, after they had led 2-1 at halftime. In fact, it was reported that "William Bly, the youthful goalkeeper who gave such a good account of himself in Third Division circles last season," had made his first wartime appearance.

City were grouped in the North Regional League in 1940-41 and played 23 games in the competition. Curnow was the goalkeeper for the first four of them, but then the club asked Bly to return to Hull. As a consequence, he moved back to East Yorkshire, where he found work with a local ship-rigger at City's request, and played in the following 16 games to the end of January 1941. His first outing was in a 3-1 home defeat by York City on September 28, 1940, when boxer Len Harvey, then the British and Empire heavyweight and light-heavyweight champion, attended the game. Bly was also in goal for the first of four Football League War Cup ties on February 15, 1941, when Bert Knott scored all the Tigers' goals in a 4-1 victory at home to Lincoln City before Curnow returned for the remaining three.

But five days after appearing in his only cuptie of the campaign Billy was given his first experience of a kind of international duty - for his country - because he was called up into the Army on February 20, 1941. John French and then David Wilson took his place in the final three North Regional League fixtures of the season as Bly began to adapt to a different kind of life.

On January 7, 1941, Billy had undergone an examination by Hull Medical Board, passing at Grade I level, and soon his certificate of registration - number WBQ 1808 - under the National Service (Armed Forces) Acts arrived. His address was given as 9 West Avenue, Hull, his height was a little more than 5ft. 9in. and his hair was said to be dark brown.

He travelled to Blackpool to enlist. His Army number was 1774865, his religious denomination was given as Church of England, his approved society was named as the Refuge Association and his trade on enlistment was a house decorator.

Bly spent nine months in the London area on a gun site at Enfield and managed to fit in some occasional regimental soccer, but eventually his service as a gunner with the Royal Artillery took him to Normandy in the Second Front. And it was not until the 1942-43 season that he began to play again on anything approaching a regular basis.

He went to Scotland, where he was with Dumbarton for three months, and on October 28, 1942, he was sent a letter by their secretary, James Denovan, who addressed him as Willie! It read: "Just a note to inform you that you have been chosen to play for the first team against Queen's Park at Boghead Park on Saturday. The kick-off is at 3pm, so please report no later than 2.30pm.

"I trust you will be able to get the necessary permission from your commanding officer. By the way, if your commanding officer is a football enthusiast, we would be more than pleased to have his company at the match.

"I have written to Hull City for their permission to play you and, up to the time of writing this note, I have had no reply. This permission is necessary before you can play, but I don't think Hull will put any restrictions in your way."

Bly also guested for Hamilton Academicals during the 1942-43 season and was involved in some remarkable games. In one they lost 8-4 to Falkirk at Brockville Park and in another they drew 4-4 against Heart of Midlothian at Tynecastle after having led 4-1 at halftime.

Billy also played one game for Lincoln City in the qualifying competition for the northern section of the Wartime Cup at home to Nottingham Forest on February 20, 1943. The Imps won 4-0, but he was unavailable for the return tie and his stay with them proved to be short-lived.

Billy was then stationed at Mushroom Farm Camp at Weathersfield in Essex and availability was a problem for him. Joe McClelland, Lincoln's secretary-manager, later wrote to him on March 7, 1943, to explain the difficulties, addressing him as Will! The letter read: "I had a very nice letter from your officer to inform me that, because of circumstances over which he had no control, it would not be possible to let you play for us at Nottingham. It was a very great disappointment. I am certain that, if you had played, we should not have had a goal against us and would, therefore, be taking part in the Cup. It has meant a loss of £500 to the club.

"I shall be very much obliged if you will keep me in touch with your movement. Then I will get you a game wherever it is possible. At present I am placing our lads all over - five with Notts County, one with Barnsley, one with Bradford. I shall be pleased to assist you to as many 30 shillings as possible because I know these little 'pick-ups' are a Godsend."

But Hull City did not forget about their promising goalkeeper either and secretary-manager Ernie Blackburn wrote to Billy at his Newcastle home from 873, Anlaby Road, on May 27, 1943. The letter read: "Now, Billy, how are you getting along? All right, I hope. No-one seems to have heard anything from you, so please drop me a line and let me know how you are getting along. The last I knew about you was that you were playing for Dumbarton a few months ago and that you seemed to be doing very well according to Press reports.

"Harold Meens is out in the Middle East - the Baghdad area - and I get letters from him now and then. He was asking me where you were these days. Jack Robinson is stationed near Huddersfield - about 12 miles from his home. Isn't he lucky? He's been there since he joined up.

up. Others are scattered all over the country and abroad.

"Glad to say that I am keeping fairly well, as is Joe Beck, who has left that shop in Walton Street and is living off Chanterlands Avenue now. He is groundsman for Tarran's Sports Club, while I have been working for the electricity department here for the past two years You know that this place has been badly knocked about and there are many buildings down.

"I shall have to send this to your home address because I don't know your unit or address in the Army. Here's wishing you all the best. All wish to be remembered to you. Cheerio, Billy."

At this time Billy was, in fact, planning to marry and on July 10, 1943, he wed Dorothy Norma Scott at St. Anthony's Church, Byker, in Newcastle. Dorothy was then 20 and she had lived at 12 Ambrose Place, Low Walker. But the marriage certificate indicated that Billy and Dorothy both lived in Walker Road at the time of the ceremony - Billy at 1,301 and Dorothy 1,327.

Amid it all, Dumbarton also remained in touch with Billy and Denovan again wrote to him on September 29, 1943: "I received your letter this morning and note your difficulty about getting in touch with me. You would get my letter, explaining the position about the two goalkeepers when your BSM wrote to me at the beginning of the season to say that you were stationed in Barrhead. My reason for getting in touch with you last week was because of injuries, etc.. I was quite sure that, if you had been available, you would have played and was also quite confident that you would have been in for so long as you were stationed in the district.

"About three weeks ago the manager of St. Mirren 'phoned me to see if I would help him regarding a goalkeeper. I gave him your name and address and he set off to try to find you, but I expect that you would be away by that time. I note that you will be back in Scotland soon. Please let me know when you return."

Billy, in fact, went to France after D-Day in 1944 and football was forgotten again. He did not play again until he was picked for the Combined Services in June 1945 and this time he regularly found himself on duty among a host of international footballers - as teammates and opponents. It was an opportunity for Billy to test himself with the best and against the best and he made the most of it.

His chance came when he was stationed in Holland and was told to report to Antwerp Stadium to play for what would become the British Army of the Rhine. They drew 1-1 against a Belgium XI and Billy reflected: "When I saw the team, it shook me because there was a whole lot of famous players, but they soon put me at my ease. Nothing would go wrong for me in my first game although I stopped the hardest shot in my life that day. It sprained both my wrists, but I held on somehow." Perhaps it was an advance warning of the injuries that were to dog him for much of his career!

On June 9, 1945, Bly played for a combined British Army and RAF team who lost 4-2 to a France Select XI at Colombes, near Paris, in front of a crowd of about 35,000. One of his teammates was England centre-forward Stan Mortensen, who was to join him at Hull City 10 years later, and a meal at the Hotel Claridge in Paris followed the game.

On July 10, 1945, Bly played for an England Professionals XI, who included internationals such as Bernard Joy, Eddie Hapgood and Jimmy Hagan, in a 2-1 win over Staevnet in Copenhagen and was even chaired off the field at the end. The BAOR team also drew 1-1 with a Danish Select XI in Copenhagen when one of Billy's opponents turned out to be Viggo Jensen, who was to be one of his teammates at Hull City when they won the Third Division North title in 1948-49.

But the team's coach Edward Bailey appreciated Bly's overall input, which was typified by the draw in Copenhagen. He observed later: "The team were virtually composed of full internationals, the exception being the goalkeeper although at this time I did have two full internationals whose services I could have called upon. But this was not necessary because Billy Bly turned in superlative performances week after week. Perhaps his finest game was in Copenhagen in 1945. We were overrun and outplayed for the greater part of the game and it was fortunate that Bly produced the sort of goalkeeping that was heralded next morning on the front pages of the Danish Press as 'the finest exhibition of goalkeeping' seen in their country.' It is most unusual for photographs of a goalkeeper to occupy the front pages of several national papers, but this is what happened. It mystified some of us after the War years how full international honours escaped Bly and I am only sorry that the FA were unable to honour him so. He was a well-liked, well-respected member of the BAOR team and his full-backs, Eddie Hapgood and Bill Hughes, both of whom had captained their countries, could not remember playing in front of a better goalkeeper."

When Bly played for the BAOR's Combined Services XI in a goalless draw against a Dutch XI in Hanover, though, his name was wrongly spelt in a newspaper cutting. He was called Bligh, which might, of course, have been sufficient to cause a mutiny! Misprints were common, in fact, because the Combined Services goalkeeper when they played Portsmouth, who included Scottish international Jimmy Scoular, at the Hindenburg Stadium in Hanover on March 13, 1946, appeared on the programme sheet as Hull of Hull City!

The Combined Services also disposed of Sheffield United, who included England international left-back Eddie Shimwell and Scotland international wing-half Alex Forbes, 5-1 and a Poland FA XI 5-0 in games in the Olympic Stadium in Berlin. On another occasion Bly sent a postcard of the stadium to Dorothy, who was staying with family in Dorset, after a game against West Ham United in October 1945. The previous March Billy and Dorothy had become parents when their daughter, Norma, had been born in Newcastle. And he wrote: "I am sending this card of the Olympic Stadium, where we played against West Ham and drew 2-2. I am sending this off before we leave Berlin today. Look after yourself and Norma, darling!"

On November 4, 1945, Bly played for the Combined Services XI (Germany) against an England FA XI at Dusseldorf Stadium. Bly's team included England internationals Leslie Compton, Tom Galley and Tim Ward and Wales right-back Bill Hughes, while they got the chance to play against an opposition including England internationals such as Bert Williams, Billy Wright, Jesse Pye, Malcolm Barrass and Willie Watson.

There was also an ironic incident involving Dai Davies, who had been a City colleague of Bly in his eight prewar League games, on the way to the match. Davies had also been selected and he recalled: "I was picked up by Army transport near Cologne to be taken to the Dusseldorf Stadium. When I got into the back of the lorry, I found that four or more players were already there and one of them was Billy Bly. As we were going along, I thought it a bit odd that Billy didn't speak to me because we had been teammates. When I eventually spoke to him, he just couldn't believe who I was. Apparently I had put on so much weight that he didn't recognise me!"

Equally incongruous was an incident involving Denis Durham, who had been a tank gunner involved in mine clearing. He was not yet a teammate of Billy at Hull City, but he had heard of him and went to watch him play for the BAOR team in Germany. But he turned up to find that Billy was not playing!

On December 13, 1945, the BAOR Combined Services faced the CMF Combined Services at the Arena in Milan and Bly opposed even more famous football names. The formidable CMF side included England internationals such as Bill Nicholson, Syd Owen, who briefly coached at Hull City in the late 1970s and appeared in the programme as Owens, and Tom Finney, Scottish international George Hamilton, Irish international "Paddy" Sloan and Welsh international Bryn Jones.

And when the BAOR beat the British Troops Austria 3-1 the same month Bly's name had again been changed: this time he had been spiritedly transformed into Blyth! The game also brought him a reunion with a current City teammate, full-back Arthur Watson, who appeared for the British Troops Austria.

On May 8, 1946, the BAOR Combined Services drew 1-1 with Fulham in Hamburg's Bahrenfeld Stadium and Bly opposed Ernie Shepherd, who returned to his native Yorkshire to join the Tigers almost three years later. The hunger for football after the austerity was evident because the game was reckoned to have attracted a crowd of about 20,000 servicemen and women.

The Combined Services squad were in Hamburg from May 6 to 9 and were treated well for the duration. On the first evening they were offered the chance to attend "Getting Around" at the Garrison Theatre or to go to the cinema. The next day involved a sight-seeing trip, including the stadium for the game, and a chance to see "Women Aren't Angels" at the Palladium. A dinner dance at Straits Hotel followed the game against Fulham the next day and the opportunity to have a massage or use the local Turkish baths or gymnasium was available before departure on May 9.

Billy was taking on the top Scots by now and possibly even giving them tips about good goalkeeping! On May 1, 1946, he played for the British Army of the Rhine in a 3-0 victory over Hibernian, who included Scottish internationals Hugh Howie, David Shaw and Gordon Smith. And on June 2 they lost 3-2 to Heart of Midlothian, who included Scottish internationals Charlie Cox, Robert Baxter, Willie Macfarlane and Tommy Walker, who moved to Chelsea three months later. Both games were played at Celle, whose ground, in fact, was known as Highbury...

On June 8, 1946, the Combined Services had a 2-2 draw against Dundee, who included Scottish international Bob Ancell, in Hamburg. And from June 24 to July 3 the BAOR Combined Services squad toured Switzerland and were based in Berne. Bly's regular international teammates included England's Leslie Compton, who normally captained the side, and Stan Rickaby, Wales' Bill Hughes and Scotland's Bill Steel.

It was at this time that Billy's exploits caught the eye of England international centre-forward Tommy Lawton, who wrote in his newspaper column: "There is such a shortage of real first-flight goalkeepers that I know that many club managers would willingly make a long trip under almost any circumstances to secure the signature of one who fills the bill. Now is the time for them to start moving because in the last few days I have seen a goalkeeper who is a natural. The name? Bly. I don't know just where, when and how he can be fixed up because he is serving with our occupation troops in Germany. I saw him pull the game out of the fire for his team when they met a Swiss XI who showed only four changes from the side who met a full England team at Stamford Bridge."

In the meantime, the 86th Heavy AA Regiment, with whom Billy served, had an outstanding soccer record between 1940 and 1946, playing 206 matches and winning 197, drawing three and losing six. And in 1940-41 they had won the AA Divisional Shield when they beat the

75th Searchlight Regiment 6-4 in the final. The following season Billy joined them and they lost only twice - to the London Scottish both times. They beat the 86th in a friendly at White Hart Lane, later to become a memorable ground for Billy in League soccer, and in the AA Divisional Shield final. Illness, though, forced Billy to miss the game.

The 86th were also successful on the Continent despite one bad spell when they lost twice and drew once in consecutive outings. They then remained unbeaten until November 1944 when they lost 6-3 to Belgian League side Aalst and it was a further 13 months before they were defeated again when they met a Yugoslavian XI in Germany.

But the 86th otherwise had a spectacular record in Germany, playing 25 matches and winning 23, drawing one and losing one. They entered the BAOR inter-unit competition under the coaching of Dave Walker and went through to win the 30 Corps Championship. They played the 1st Border Regiment at Osnabruck in the final on March 24, 1946, and won 3-2. It was 1-1 at halftime after both sides had scored penalties and then the 86th had to come from behind, missing a second penalty along the way. And it was reported in Shrapnel, the regimental magazine: "The 3-2 victory was well-deserved on the run of play and Bly was his usual confident self in goal."

Edward Heath, later to become the Prime Minister and be awarded a knighthood, had become second-in-command and commanding officer of the 86th Regiment of the Honourable Artillery Company in the autumn of 1945 and given high priority to producing a successful soccer team. His industry paid off because the 86th duly reached the British Army of the Rhine Inter-Unit Championship final, beating the East Riding Yeomanry 3-1 in Hamburg on March 27, 1946, at the semi-final stage when Billy took a knock in the first half.

It meant that the 86th Honourable Artillery Company's Heavy AA Regiment, who were the winning unit of 30 Corps District, met the 45th RHU (Malines), the winning unit of L. of C. Troops in the final over two legs. The first leg was played at Wembley Stadium, Osnabruck, on March 31, 1946, and Billy's team won 2-1 even though he had been taken ill on the morning of the match. The second leg was played at Malines in Belgium on Sunday, April 7, and a goalless draw was sufficient to give the 86th the championship.

Mr. Heath was always willing to praise Billy's goalkeeping ability and they did, in fact, have two memorable reunions in later years. The first came when he was Minster of Labour during Billy's last season with Hull City and again when he toured Hull's Fish Dock as the Leader of the Opposition in September 1968. Mr. Heath recalled on the first occasion: "The regiment were soccer-mad and we became divisional champions, corps champions and finally Rhine Army champions while Bill was our goalkeeper." Billy audaciously observed that Mr. Heath looked a "a bit greyer and more prosperous" since their last meeting in those days and admitted that their only contact in-between had been by means of exchanging Christmas cards.

Billy, meanwhile, had been released from the Army at the Infantry Barracks in York on July 27, 1946, after peace has finally been restored and his trade was given as an equipment repairer when he left the Royal Artillery. He had to decide what to do about his future, but initially soccer was not at the top of his list of priorities. In fact, there was a short period when it looked as if he might be lost to the game as a whole and not just Hull City. Billy recalled: "I came near to packing up on demobilisation when I had a decorating business in Newcastle for a brief spell. But I felt the call and I signed for Hull City again after ironing out a few personal matters with Maj. Frank Buckley, who was manager of the reorganised club at the new Boothferry Park ground. I am glad I did, too, because those boom years at Hull immediately after the War were an experience I would not have missed for anything."

5

Safe Keeping

Billy Bly's wartime activities had at least enabled him to gain some further experience as a goalkeeper in good company. But all football had become fragmented as he switched from occasional outings with Hull City to guest appearances for various other clubs and then to the success with the British Army of the Rhine. There was little doubt that stability was badly needed in all walks of life, but the Tigers scarcely provided it because they were undergoing significant changes in different directions.

As the plans for the return to structured League soccer were taking shape everywhere, Billy had to adjust to new surroundings with City because they had left their prewar Anlaby Road ground to move to their new stadium a mile or so further out of the city centre at Boothferry Park. And it had also been made possible by a boardroom reshuffle.

There was also a change at management level because Ernie Blackburn, the secretary-manager who had signed Billy and then given him his League baptism as a teenager, was no longer in office. Blackburn, who had been in charge at Wrexham when the Tigers appointed him towards the end of 1936 after protracted negotiations, had had some success on the field while repeatedly having to deal delicately with an awkward financial situation. But he had done much of his rebuilding work, mixing experienced players, non-League recruits and youngsters such as Bly, when war broke out. Most of that squad, though, were no longer available in the aftermath of the War and Blackburn was not going to get the chance to find out because the new board ruthlessly ousted him early in 1946. He was installed as Tranmere Rovers' manager later in the year, but City replaced him with Maj. Frank Buckley, a Mancunian who had made one appearance for England in 1914 as a centre-half. Buckley had been forced to end his playing career after being wounded at the Battle of the Somme in 1916 during the First World War, but he had then managed Norwich City, Blackpool and Wolverhampton Wanderers during peacetime football. He had briefly taken charge of Notts County during the Second World War before the Tigers' new regime appointed him in May 1946 at the age of 63.

Billy Bly also had to adjust to a radical change of playing personnel as the Tigers prepared for the 1946-47 season. They were to use an amazing 43 players during the campaign - reckoned to be the then third-highest complement ever in British League soccer - but most of them had not previously played for the club. In fact, the 43 contained only three survivors from Blackburn's 1938-39 first-teamers - Bly, his close friend Harold Meens and Dai Davies, whose brother-in-law Ernie Bell, however, returned for a second spell with the club.

But Bly soon made an impact as City started out life at Boothferry Park. He had played in only the first four matches of the 1946-47 campaign when he found himself to be the centre of attention because it was disclosed that Buckley had turned down a bid of £12,000 for him and inside-forward Frank McGorrighan from a First Division club.

There had also been a change of outlook with regard to Bly's immediate postwar playing terms because they improved considerably. Buckley offered him £7 10s. per week from August 1, 1946, to August 30, 1946, and then £10 per week from August 31 - the first day of the new season and the start of a new era at Boothferry Park - until May 3, 1947. Bly was also offered "all bonuses" as he began a season in League soccer for the first time. It is curious that the last five games were played after May 3 because the season did not finish until June 7, but there was an added bonus that Billy, Davies and Meens, the three survivors from the final full prewar season, were the recipients of cheques for their service at a civic presentation dinner organised by City at Hull Guildhall on May 19. This time Billy's address in his contract, which was not signed by a witness, was given as 190 Church Street, Walker. It was also the address given in his national registration identity card on July 29, 1946, because he and Dorothy had moved into a flat there after their wedding in July 1943. It proved to be very handy because Dorothy, like Billy, came from a large family and she and her sister Hilda, who now lives in a flat in the Benton area of Newcastle, were very close. Hilda and Florrie, another sister, had been bridesmaids at Billy and Dorothy's wedding and Hilda had spent a lot of time with Dorothy while Billy was away in the Army, at one stage helping her with baby Norma. But Billy, Dorothy and Norma eventually moved out of the flat following his demobilisation.

Billy had plenty of addresses at the time. He briefly moved to 60 Plane Street off Anlaby Road in West Hull in August 1946 and the following month he and his family went into lodgings a relatively-short distance away at 9 Brougham Street off Albert Avenue. Billy played in half of City's Third Division North games in 1946-47 amid some injury lay-offs and the following season the club in effect paid him less! His next contract, by the time of which he had moved into one of City's club houses at 60 Worcester Road, Wold Road, Hull, was from June 12, 1947, to July 31, 1948, and offered him £9 a week during the playing season "as defined by the League and FA" and £8 a week during the close season. He was again awarded bonuses "as allowed by the League" and offered £1 a match extra when he was in the first team. Whether the arrangement was directly a result of Billy's injury problems and the club decided to insert a pay-as-you-play clause is open to debate, but Roy Bly suggested: "I don't think that my dad would have thought about it that way. He would just have got on with it." As it was, Billy made 27 League appearances in 1947-48 and the situation changed when Raich Carter became manager.

The contract for the 1948-49 season was naturally the first one to include the joint signatures of Bly and Carter and it was more straightforward to the extent that it did not distinguish between in-season and out-of-season considerations. Billy was simply paid £10 a week from August 1, 1948, to July 31, 1949, but he would get £12 a week if he were in the first team in addition to the customary bonuses. Billy, in fact, missed only four games in all as the Tigers swept to the Third Division North title.

But even though City were playing at the higher Second Division level in 1949-50, it made no difference to him financially. He remained on exactly the same terms, so winning promotion brought more kudos than monetary benefit. This time, though, the arrangement was not made between the manager and the player because it was signed by director Dick Smith, who doubled up as secretary, instead of Carter.

By 1950-51 Billy's terms were back on a dual basis. He was given a pay rise to £12 a week from August 1, 1950, to May 19, 1951 - a fortnight after the final game of the season - and then he was paid £10 a week from May 20 to the end of July 1951. The fact that on this occasion he was not paid extra for being in the first team was to his advantage because he had only five senior outings throughout the season because of injuries. There was a further bonus - in addition to the usual ones - in that, "subject to the sanction of the Football League, a benefit of £750 will be paid after completing five full playing seasons."

City, doubtless, thought that it was beneficial to put Billy back on to an agreement that included a bonus for first-team appearances because of his unavailability for much of 1950-51. And that is just what they did do the following season while the basic terms remained the same - £12 a week during the season and £10 a week from May 4, 1952, until the end of June. But Billy was also offered £14 a week when he was in the first team and he duly obliged by playing 34 out of the 42 League games. The contract was now signed by secretary Cyril Lee, whose address was given as 99 Boothferry Road, Hull.

The terms remained the same for the 1952-53 campaign when Billy again played in half of the League games. The adjustment was that the close-season figure was implemented for the whole of July 1952 because his previous deal had expired at the end of June. The same figures and adjustments applied in 1953-54 when Billy played in 26 League matches and six out of City's seven FA Cup ties, but then came another pay rise.

The wage for appearances was again waived, but Billy was given two increases. During the 1954-55 season he was paid £15 a week and during July 1954 and the 1955 close season he received £12 a week. There were two new clauses, concerning illness and injury and the degree of his payment in certain circumstances, in the contract and Billy responded by playing in 27 League games.

The terms - without the added clauses - remained the same for 1955-56 when Billy played in 26 League games in a season in which City were relegated from the Second Division. One minor alteration was that the witness for the contract was manager Bob Brocklebank in this instance.

Relegation back to the Third Division North brought changes to the terms of Billy's contract for the 1956-57 season. The two extra clauses returned for another season and the seasonal adjustments again disappeared. This time he was paid a basic £12 a week throughout the campaign from July 1, 1956, to June 30, 1957, but the advantage was that he remained on £15 a week when he was in the first team and he played in 40 League games out of 46 and all three FA Cup ties.

Billy's terms were the same for 1957-58 - although the clauses were again removed - and he made a loss on the previous season because he played in only 26 League games and three out of five FA Cup ties. But the clauses reappeared the following season and there were the most drastic changes to one of Billy's contracts as there ever had been during his long stay with City.

Whether those additional terms made any difference to the overall approach is unlikely, but they did coincide with a promotion season in 1958-59. Billy, whose address was given as his shop at 33 Boothferry Road, Hull, for the first time, was on £14 a week throughout from the start of July 1958 to the end of June 1959 and he also accepted £17 a week when he was on first-team duty. But there was a further schedule of increases in addition to those two pay rises and for the first time it applied to attendances, bearing in mind that it was the first season in which the Third Division was deregionalised, so there was fewer opportunities for derby games. Billy was given an extra £1 a week for gates of more than 14,000, £2 a week for gates of more than 17,000 and £3 a week for attendances of more than 20,000. There was a further rider: "These increases shall apply to home and away matches and in no week shall the maximum wage exceed £20."

It probably seemed to be a relatively-safe investment for the Tigers because they had been watched by crowds of more then 14,000 for only two out of their 46 League games in the Third Division North during 1957-58 - both at Boothferry Park. They had 17,761 against York City on the opening day and 16,763 against Bradford City on Easter Monday - two days after they had trounced Oldham Athletic 9-0 in their biggest League win in Billy's time at the club.

Ironically, they had been watched by crowds of between 14,338 and 51,834 in five of their six F.A. Cup ties.

But City paid the price in Billy's case in 1958-59 because the Tigers won promotion and naturally attendances increased in tandem. For example, there were 14,318 fans present for the first game of the season at home to Plymouth Argyle, the eventual champions, and an attendance of 20,238 for the return game at Home Park in mid-season. Furthermore, City attracted two other notable attendances at Boothferry Park - 20,836 for their 5-2 win over Mansfield Town on Boxing Day, 1958, and 24,156 for their 3-3 draw against Norwich City, who had reached the FA Cup semi-finals, on Easter Saturday, 1959.

It is odd that City found themselves in financial trouble when they released Billy at the end of the 1959-60 season following relegation from the Second Division, but the crowd bonuses had not applied on this occasion. He did receive pay rises as a reward for promotion, but his contract showed merely £17 a week from July 1, 1959, to June 30, 1960, and £20 when he was in the first team.

The wages appear minimal in comparison with modern times, but occasionally there were other means of increasing income. Fellow goalkeeper Bernard Fisher recalled: "Billy and I worked together with two or three other players for two weeks during one summer to help groundsman Stan Coombs to seed the pitch. It was to help to supplement our wages, which were not so good in those days."

But Billy would never have had so many contracts in the first place if he had not set himself high standards. That involved professionalism and dedication, working hard at his game and developing habits that would always stand him in good stead.

Roy Bly explained: "Being a professional footballer was a dream come true for my father. He loved playing, but I do know that he used to work hard in training. He used to punish himself at times and he used to work really hard at things that looked natural to anybody else who saw him play. Physically he used to push his body to the limits so that he could perform well.

"He had to do something to build himself up because I believe that he weighed only about nine stone at the age of 18. He was very lightweight in his younger days and people kept writing him off because they didn't think that such a skinny, young man could play the goalkeeper's role. He was put on steaks and all sorts, but eventually he did start to put some weight on.

"It was just one of those things. Football clubs had only basic facilities in those days and he didn't have some of the modern equipment, so the medicine ball played a big part in helping him to build up his strength. He used to use one a lot and work a lot on his stomach. He would be on his back and people would throw the medicine ball to him. He'd have to sit up and catch it and throw it back. Then he would lie back down. It was the same as sit-ups, but with a medicine ball. But a lot of young people now might not even know what a medicine ball was.

"And in those days there was Bunker's Hill behind one goal before they built the South Stand and redeveloped Boothferry Park. It was very high and a very steep climb and people nowadays wouldn't believe the number of steps there were on it. But dad did a lot of jogging and he used to sprint up and down the steps and do exercises on the barriers.

"I always remember my dad being quite fit, but it was amazing how he used to skip. He had a skipping-rope as part of his routine and he would skip at speed. He would also cross his hands, turning the rope and skipping back through it. He became a specialist at it and I think it helped his quick thinking as a goalkeeper.

"Above all, he used to work hard at what he did. He used to put himself through it physically and he used to maintain his routines."

One of Billy's training routines received publicity during the 1948-49 promotion season - the idea of throwing "spinners" at a wall in order to make a goalkeeper catch unpredicatble rebounds. Another one was even more strange. Bob Dennison, one of Billy's City teammates in the 1950s, recalled: "He used to sit under the hot tap in the team bath in the dressing-room and just let the scalding water run down his back and all over him. The tap was like a hose, which was about three or four inches in diameter, so it used to come out at a fair pace, but Billy didn't seem to mind. Then he'd just come and sit with the rest of us in the water that was at a normal temperature. I don't know whether he did it to try to make himself more supple in some way, but it made the rest of us cringe! But one of the trainers, Fred Smith, who was a big fellow, used to plonk himself in the little bath of cold water that was at the side of the main bath and it used to splash everywhere off him, so maybe it all evened itself out for Billy in the end."

There was one ritual, though, that caused a mixture of controversy and merriment when Billy rebelled against change in the late 1950s. Roy Bly explained: "The players used to loosen up and warm up by running round the outside perimeter of the pitch at Boothferry Park. They'd sprint and they'd run three sides and then walk the other side. But my dad had always done it on his own and he did it his way, which included running his way round. But when Gus McLean took over as coach, he tried to make him do it the other way round. Dad was a creature of habit and he was strange in that way, but he used to run round anti-clockwise in training. His attitude was: 'I've done it for years, so I'm going to continue doing it this way and I'm not going to do it any other way.' But Gus put the players into certain groups for them to run round. He blew a whistle for them to start and two of the players went one way while my dad went the other! When my dad got back, Gus said to him: 'What do you think you're playing at?' My dad asked what he meant and Gus replied that he was supposed to go off with the others. My dad told him: 'Look, I've been doing this for 20 years and this is the way I've always done it. If you've got any problems with it, then go and see Harold Needler.' But that was the way my dad was. If he did have an opinion, he would always give it."

Billy's teammate and good friend Brian Bulless recalled how the incident had far-reaching implications: "One morning we ran on to the track to do so many laps around the ground and we lined up in pairs behind each other as we had always done for years. We always ran the same way round - anti-clockwise - but we were all amused to see Bill running the opposite way on his own. Bob Brocklebank was quickly brought out of his office on to the track, but no amount of pleading could change Bill's direction."

Winger Charlie Crickmore remembered that the conversation between McLean and Billy caused great hilarity: "Angus said: 'You will do it.' Billy replied: 'I won't do it.' Billy ran round his way and I seem to remember Angus saying that he would get the manager if that were his attitude. But Billy was very superstitious, dug his heels in and said that it was his lucky way. Angus then replied: 'You've broken nearly every bone in your body. How can you talk about having luck?' We couldn't laugh about it at the time, but it was very funny."

Inside-forward Dave King also recalled the incident with great fondness: "Billy liked his routines and he wouldn't change from one which, he felt, had stood him in good stead. I think his actual words were: 'I'm sorry, but my legs won't do it!'"

And goalkeeper Bernard Fisher recalled that Billy had triumphed in his war of words with McLean about his ritual: "For some reason that morning Billy came out just after we'd started and began running the normal way before he was told to run the other. His reply was: 'I've run this way for 20 years and I'm not changing now.' This nearly started a war - much to the amusement of all the other players. Billy trained on his own for two weeks and was the butt of many jokes from everyone. In the end, though, it all settled down to allow Bill to go his way round the ground, but I can still laugh about it."

Billy believed in good habits and regimentation and he once explained: "The discipline started in the clubs and there was no mucking about - even before the War. You had a dressing-room for the first team and all the others went into the other dressing-room and you daren't go in among the first team. If you were, say, playing darts or snooker and a first-team player wanted to play, he went on and you came off. You did as you were told."

Dave King backed up the philosophy: "People looked up to Billy because he believed in doing things properly. He always felt that you should carry yourself in the right way and, whenever I walked past the shop that he had near the ground, I stood up straight as I went by and made sure that I didn't look as if I were slouching just in case he saw me!

"He also believed in people knowing their place. When I first got into the first team and was allowed to use the home dressing-room, I got into the bath and sat in the corner one day. But Billy told me to move because his bottom had made a rim in that corner for years and it was his place!"

As Billy developed as a goalkeeper, he knew what he wanted and what he needed. He might have been a creature of habit, but his aim always was to be in a position in which he could satisfactorily meet the demands of being a professional goalkeeper. Most of his preparation and routines were designed to help his mobility and flexibility, to enable him to be in command of what he was doing and to aid his chances of coping with the physical pressures.

Billy worked hard to earn his reputation as the so-called India Rubber Man although he did insist: "I don't get this acrobatic business from having watched Continentals. I just do it naturally. It is the only way that I can get at a ball to get my body right behind it."

His suppleness, though, was appreciated by his teammates. Winger Mike Bowering pointed out: "Billy was so elastic in his movement, but he was also a very good sprinter and people didn't always appreciate how quick he was." And Jack Bennion, a wing-half and long-throw expert, whose father, Ray, had been a Welsh international, said: "I got on extremely well with Billy. He was the most agile person I've known. He could twist himself and must have been double-jointed all over. He hated being beaten by a lob over his head after he'd come out to narrow the angle - even in training. He was unbelievable in training because of some of the exercises he did. He was so supple. He could twist himself all the way round for some of them when the rest of us could go only halfway round - yet we were all supposed to be fit."

Bly's bravery as a goalkeeper was also second-to-none. It may have brought him some of his injuries, but he always felt that it was a fundamental element of doing his job properly. And full-back Mike Brown summed it up neatly: "Billy was very brave and probably broke most of the bones in his body at some time, but he was still a very good 'keeper."

Defender Brian Garvey, a regular in City's 1958-59 promotion side alongside Billy, said: "He was the oldest player in that team and I was the youngest, but I respected him a lot. I played as a part-timer for Hull City when I first joined the club, so I didn't train a lot with players such as Billy, but I do remember that he wasn't tall. Nowadays people seem to expect every goalkeeper to be at least 6ft. 3in. tall, but it didn't matter as much in our day. Billy was slightly-built compared with a lot of goalkeepers, but he was very agile and brave. In those days forwards could go in and charge the goalkeepers when they had the ball. It wasn't like it is nowadays when the goalkeepers are protected so much, so they had to be brave to stand up to it. But it didn't stop Billy from doing his job of a goalkeeper because he was very acrobatic. When you played in front of Billy, you still had confidence in him as a goalkeeper because he was always positive and willing to come out for things."

Inside-forward Norman Wilkinson played only eight games for the Tigers during the autumn of 1953 before making a name for himself with York City. He also came from the North-East - from Alnwick - and he recalled a 2-0 defeat away to Everton when Bly's courage was ruthlessly put to the test: "They had a centre-forward called Dave Hickson, who was a bit of a crackerjack, and he caused some bad feeling because he clattered into Billy after he'd gone down with the ball. But Billy just got on with it because he was fearless."

Roy Bly realised that his father could also look after himself because he said: "He told me that in one game he was playing against Brian Clough, who crocked him. My dad got a right knock from him and later in the game he got him back, as professionals do sometimes, because he went up to defend himself with his knees high. He caught Cloughy in his back or side and didn't injure him. But it was mainly to protect himself and it was also to say: 'Eh, mate, two can play at this game.'"

Winger Doug Clarke, an awesome striker of a football, remembered Billy's philosophy of defiance: "He was a top-flight goalkeeper. He was always a good trainer, rising to the challenge laid down by the faster guys. On cold and wet winter days he would arrive back from training covered from head to toe in mud. As for the idea that I tested Billy out in training because I had a hard shot, bigger names than I found him fearless, agile and very difficult to beat.

"I always felt that, when in many cases he became the last line of our defence, it was no easy task for our opponents because they had to pass Bill, who was completely fearless and in a number of instances came out of it all with quite a few nasty injuries."

An important factor was that Bly's approach instilled confidence in those immediately in front of him. Denis Durham, a left-back or left-half, was one of his closest friends, as was Harold Meens, and he said: "First and foremost we felt much safer having Bill behind us. We covered each other where possible in the event of errors, but Bill was so reliable. A great strength he had was going for crosses from any position, be it a free-kick, a corner or a cross from the wing. The six-yard box was his territory: it was his ground. Goalkeepers were expected to be dominant in their six-yard boxes and Bill was certainly that. He was a fearless goalkeeper, always going off his line and diving at the opposition forwards' feet and often getting injured in the process. But that was Bill - a great goalkeeper. I've no doubt in my mind that he would have gone on to receive international honours if he had kept free from injury."

Roy echoed the sentiment: "Dad always maintained that the six-yard box was his. I think he was commanding in it verbally and he always said that you were a weak goalkeeper if you weren't. I don't think that my father was loud or extrovert as a goalkeeper, but I think he used to let people know what he expected. I think he just transferred his normal personality into a game, but maybe he was a bit assertive in his role as a goalkeeper in that six-yard box."

Above all, it was a professional attitude and Andy Davidson, who joined City's ground staff in 1948 and remains the club's record appearances holder despite some injury setbacks of his own, got a memorable taste of it as a youngster: "The first time that I met Billy was during my trial with Hull City when I played in the reserves against the first team in their practice match on Boothferry Park. The trial was going okay, but things looked really good when Harold

Meens let me past him into the 18-yard box. I thought: 'I'm going to score against the first team.' I looked up to pick my spot when something shot between my legs. It was Billy. No way was a novice going to score against him, but that was Billy. If you were going to beat him, it was on merit, not sympathy."

And City's other goalkeepers might have been Billy's rivals, but they also knew that they could learn a lot from his dedication and routines. They knew that they could pick up useful tips just by watching him and following his example. Some, such as Ron Capewell and Barry Lord, were based outside the area and did not get to know him as well as others such as Bernard Fisher and Len Round, who openly admit to having benefited from learning a lot from Billy.

Fisher, who worked with Billy from 1955 to 1960 before succeeding him as the Tigers' first-choice goalkeeper, recalled: "When training, I was always alongside Billy from running to exercising in the visitors' dressing-room on our own at times. We had a suspended punch-ball, like those that the boxers use, in one corner and Billy was excellent with it. He taught me how to use it and it was good for training and co-ordination. In training Billy was one of the fastest sprinters, in particular over the first 50 yards, and again this was very good for goalkeepers.

"Billy, to this day, was the best 'keeper I've seen at going into a one-to-one and diving at a player's feet and you had to be very good to beat him. A great catcher of crossed balls, he was a strong believer in catching with punching being a last resort. He also hated being beaten by shots from the edge of the penalty area and was horrified to be beaten from 25 yards or more whether it be in a match of practice."

Round, who spent just one season with the Tigers in 1957-58 and made 17 first-team appearances, observed: "I had come down to have a go with Hull City from Ayr United, where I had been for more than 10 years. I trained with Billy and Bernard Fisher and I learned more from Billy Bly in one season than I had at Ayr in 10! After I left Hull City, I went down to Kent to play non-League for Sittingbourne and I went there a better goalkeeper than ever!

"I remember that Billy always seemed to get the ball when he dived down to get it at a player's feet and I didn't. Billy told me that I was going out too fast, so we would practise and talk about it and it made me a better goalkeeper. And in those days the balls were heavier and laced and I also remember that Billy showed me how to punch them better.

"In training Billy would always be able to jump up the steps on the terraces at Boothferry Park three or four at a time and I could manage only two or three. Yet I remember one Friday morning when we went out to jump the steps and Billy slipped and badly cut his knee open. Billy was out of action for some time and it led to another opportunity for me to play in the first team!"

And when City signed Les Green, another small goalkeeper by most modern standards, from his home-town club Atherstone Town as a 19-year-old in 1960, he soon realised that he would have to go on a pilgrimage to make the most of his opportunity to establish himself in League soccer. He was in digs with the Ness family on Boothferry Road near to the Tigers' ground - and, equally importantly, Billy's sweet shop, which he visited in order to learn the skills of goalkeeping.

He recalled: "How could I turn down a chance to learn from Billy Bly? I had read about him as a kid and he was a star among stars. Anyone who wanted to make it in League football and was a goalkeeper modelled himself on Billy Bly because he had been there and done it all.

"He taught me so much and the experience that he passed on was invaluable, but that's what happened in those days. People in specialist positions would pass on their knowledge and advice and it was a pleasure to be in Billy's company. He could have played for any club in the country, but decided to be a one-club man."

Green made only four senior appearances for the Tigers and became unsettled when he was promised a club house and then found that Dudley Price had been given one before him. Green, who was on £12 a week with a £20 bonus for being in the first team, was in effect tied and owned by City, so he opted to return to non-League soccer with Nuneaton Borough and Burton Albion. He then had spells at Hartlepools United and Rochdale before Brian Clough took him to Derby County, where he was an ever-present when they easily won the old Second Division title in 1968-69 and then established himself in the First Division.

Green added: "Billy told me: 'Les, you will go on greater things - greater than what I have achieved.' When Brian Clough, who had been my manager at Hartlepools, signed me again, I went on to my most successful period in soccer at Derby and things worked out just as Billy had told me they would."

And when Billy became a shopkeeper only a few yards from Boothferry Park in the late 1950s, it had a profound effect on City's training methods, notoriously taking them on to a far more competitive level than before. Roy Bly explained: "When he began running his sweets and confectionery shop, dad had an old case that looked like something that the Chancellor of the Exchequer would use for the budget and I always remember him filling it up with a fair few things such as Mars Bars. The story goes that the players used to have five-a-sides in training when there used to be cinders on the car-park at the front of Boothferry Park and got a bit of a competition going. I remember that there was a notebook in the case and he used to mark off with a tick who had paid for what. The winning team only used to get the Mars Bars, but I think that in the end dad used to give them away."

Colin Smith backed up the procedure: "We used to have five-a-side games in training and Billy, who had taken over a sweet shop in readiness for when he retired, would supply us with a very good choice of chocolate bars from a case that he carried." And Brian Bulless added: "When Bill had a sweet shop, he would bring in a suitcase full of items such as sweets, chocolates and chewing gum on training days. The lads would help themselves after training and then pay Bill. Although there was just a mass of bodies helping themselves from the case in the dressing-room, Bill always seemed to know exactly who owed what."

Bernard Fisher remembered the cut-throat nature of training as City players fought over the spoils of Billy's case: "Once he had the shop, he would bring his little brown case to training and sell chocolate. He would give a Mars Bar each to the winning five-a-side team during training when games were fiercely contested just for the prize." And Mike Brown added: "One of the best things I remember is Billy bringing in a little case to training every morning. It was stacked and contained everything from cigarettes to Mars Bars. We would play games for five-a-sides for a Mars Bar a man and we'd get battered. The losers had to pay out and you'd kill for a Mars Bar. Andy Davidson and I were always fighting over Billy's Mars Bars on the car-park and we'd ended up being taken to see the manager. But I always blamed Billy for it!"

Whether the contents of Billy's case actually played an integral role in helping to propel the Tigers to promotion from the Third Division in 1958-59 is open to conjecture. They added a serious note in terms of the increased competitiveness in training, but they also produced a dark humour at times because they were never far off from being sacrosanct. Charlie Crickmore explained: "We'd play in five-a-sides in training and the losers would pay for the Mars Bars from Billy. But on one occasion, when Joe Stocks, Dave King and I were ground-staff lads, we hid Billy's box of tricks in the treatment room and he went berserk. In the end we had to tell him what we'd done because we knew it had gone too far. I used to call him 'Dad' and he would say: 'Less of your lip, son!' But it was all just a joke with him."

And it was not just Billy's application to setting his own goalkeeping standards season after season that impressed his teammates. His friendliness and attitude towards them were much appreciated. By the 1950s he was one of City's senior professionals and his natural warmth and generosity of spirit towards his younger, up-and-coming colleagues were very welcome.

Charlie Crickmore: "I had a lot of affection for him. We took the same size in boots and we had to buy our own when we were on the ground staff, so Billy gave me a pair of his old ones. But he had boots that were specially built up for him for goalkeeping and didn't wear the traditional ones. I daren't refuse him or tell him that Brian Cripsey had already given me a pair of his.

"Billy always changed in his own spot in the dressing-room and he was a very competitive bloke. He was also a very good player when he played out of goal in training. But I thought he was brilliant as a goalkeeper, especially his positional play, and it was easy to see why the general public thought so much about him after he had played all those years for the same club."

Forward Dave Fraser recalled: "Billy and Viggo Jensen were fantastic because they always spoke to younger players. They encouraged me, which others did, but not in the way that Bill and Viggo did. They looked after you like father figures and went out of their way to make sure you were all right. I can't speak about them highly enough because you don't seem to get that nowadays."

Full-back Johnny Neal, who went on to have a successful career in football management, enjoyed the support that he received from Billy both on and off the field: "My father was a staunch churchgoer and, when Sunderland wanted me, he kept to his word because he had promised Hull City that I would sign for them. And, looking back, it was the best thing that ever happened to me in football because I was among great, great professionals at Hull and I got an amazing grounding with them.

"Billy was a good servant and it was also good to listen to him and learn from him. He was very light and frail-looking, but he was very brave. In fact, he was the bravest I've seen. I played at the back with people such as Billy and Neil Franklin, who had enormous experience. And when we played away, they looked after me because they were great professionals and great personalities.

"It was great to have players such as Billy, Raich Carter, Andy Davidson, Gerry Bowler, Wilf Hassall and Viggo Jensen to show me and advise me. They taught me principles and ideals as a player. They were good players and lovely people with great morals, so what more could anyone ask?"

Billy Bly had come a long way and had made his mark in different ways - as a dedicated, well-ordered professional who worked diligently at trying to perfect the art of goalkeeping and as a benevolent, big-hearted man who willingly helped his colleagues whenever he could. And Hull City fans had been grateful that more often than not their last line of defence was in Billy's safe keeping.

6

Bones of Contention

Billy Bly was closely associated with both fitness and injury in a bizarre kind of way. His elasticity and agility suggested that he was a fitness fanatic and provided him with his nickname of the India Rubber Man, but he was also known variously as being either a raw-boned or brittle-boned hero. The descriptions stemmed from a long run of injuries that disrupted his career at regular intervals and forced him to endure numerous spells on the sidelines.

He earned a reputation for being injury-prone, but, if that is a criticism, then it also has to be remembered that he had the courage to bounce back resiliently and repeatedly. Bly may have suffered relentlessly for his art, but he played League soccer until he was nearly 40 and it was age rather than injury that finally prompted Hull City not to renew his contract. If he were courageous on the pitch, then he was equally fearless in his determination to beat injuries off it. He may have been unlucky to the extent that he nearly always seemed to suffer serious injuries, but he accepted them as part and parcel of the game and a testimony to his style of goalkeeping that so often bordered on the excesses of bravery.

Billy Bly spent a sporting lifetime trying to defy the odds because the curious aspect of it all is that he might never have been encouraged to take up a career that owed so much to physical contact in the first place. At the same time he might also have been discouraged from being a goalkeeper because he was not the biggest and well-built player of his type.

His son, Roy, put it into perspective: "In his youth my dad took a year off because he had a damaged ankle. He had weak ankles and used to get pain from them. I think the brittle bones came because of the kind of consistent injuries that he had over the years. You then start to think that something's wrong and he must have had brittle bones. But maybe that might have happened to anybody."

Bernard Fisher, one of Bly's goalkeeping colleagues at Boothferry Park, added: "Pet names I remember for him are 'Brittle-bone Bly' and 'Dare-devil Bly.' He came to training with a broken toe one day, saying that he had done it turning over in bed! He did a training exercise, which was to see how many terrace steps he could leap up from a standing jump near the tunnel leading to the pitch at Boothferry Park. One day he slipped while doing it and gashed his knee badly. I said to him on his return a week or so later: 'You won't try that again.' But typically Billy did and slipped again. Luckily there was no damage and he was okay."

Injuries, in fact, played a major part in Bly's career from the outset. In fact, he was hurt during a wartime match away to Halifax Town in the North Regional League on November 9, 1940. City were losing 1-0 when Bly flung himself bravely at the feet of the incoming Stan Wood, who looked certain to score, and received a leg injury. He continued briefly, but had to go off shortly before halftime with Dai Davies taking over in goal as the Tigers played on with 10 men, finally going down 3-0.

On another wartime occasion he was injured in the British Army of the Rhine Inter-Unit Shield semi-final in Hamburg in March 1946 when helping the 86th Heavy AA Regiment to a 3-1 win over the East Riding Yeomanry. The 86th were coming under pressure after taking a 1-0 lead in the 12th minute and it was reported: "The Yeomanry pressed for some time and during one of their raids Bly had the misfortune to cut the skin above his eye when making a save, but he kept his goal intact."

When organised soccer resumed after the 1939-45 War, City moved from Anlaby Road to Boothferry Park, where they first played a League game in the old Third Division North against Lincoln City on August 31, 1946. It ended in a goalless draw in front of a crowd of 25,586 on a wet afternoon and the Tigers were hit by injuries. Ernie Bell suffered concussion when he was hit in the face by a clearance after 20 minutes although he returned in the second half. And, as ambulancemen were kept busy taking care of fans who fainted, they had to break off to attend to Bly when he collided with Lincoln's Harry Parr and had to be carried off on a stretcher. He was unable to return and full-back Arthur Watson had to take over from him in goal although Bly had recovered sufficiently to take his place in City's line-up for their next game two days later - a 2-2 home draw against Crewe Alexandra.

Bly played in the first nine games of the season, beating the eight in succession that he had played after his prewar debut, but then disaster struck again. City won 3-1 away to Tranmere Rovers after a coach journey lasting about six-and-a-half hours on October 5. The Tigers' centre-forward Benny Lester led the way with a hat-trick, but Bly had to make a number of pointblank saves and in one instance he was kicked on his right thumb, which was dislocated and later found out to have been broken. He continued, but it was thought that he might have saved Tranmere's goal by Kinear Burns but for the injury. Ironically, Rovers were by then managed by Ernie Blackburn, who had, of course, been responsible for bringing Billy to Hull in the first place. Billy later reflected: "A through ball came towards goal, I rushed out to whip it away from an attacker, his boot pushed my thumb back and I had my first break."

Cyril Hannaby deputised in goal for City in the next seven games before Bly himself returned for a run of seven League matches. His return, though, coincided with the start of the FA Cup, in which City needed two games to dispose of New Brighton in the first round. And Bly was subjected to what was regarded as special treatment in an attempt to get him fit for the first meeting - he had a gruelling training session against Harold Meens and Arthur Watson, "two of the club's strongest kickers!" He eventually played in four FA Cup ties, but contracted mumps after the last one - a 1-1 draw at First Division Blackburn Rovers in the third round on January 11, 1947. It meant that Joe Carter played in the replay, which City lost 3-0 in front of a 30,501 crowd, the biggest so far at Boothferry Park. Carter, curiously, had fractured his wrist shortly after Bly had suffered his thumb injury and had only just returned to action. It was his debut for the Tigers and he also played in the next five League games - his only first-team appearances for the club - before Bly returned.

Billy was back in the first team in mid-March for five more League games until he was injured again in what had turned out to be a stop-start season for him. On April 5 City won 2-1 away to Oldham Athletic during the three-match Easter programme with goals by David Davidson and Bly suffered a broken finger. In the end he stayed on in the second half when his colleagues protected him as much as possible although City's manager Maj. Frank Buckley came up with his own novel way of protecting his goalkeeper. Billy recalled: "Seeing my trouble, he broke all the teeth from a hair comb and bound the stem round the finger. The referee failed to spot it and I played for the whole 90 minutes." But the injury was still enough to rule him out of the final nine games of the season as the Tigers finished 11th in the Third Division North.

Billy began the 1947-48 campaign as City's first-choice goalkeeper - Carter had moved to the then Bournemouth and Boscombe Athletic - and played in the opening 11 League matches, but then he demonstrated his capacity for getting injured any time and anywhere. This time it was in training. It may well have been thought that David Beckham "invented" the broken metatarsal bone in his left foot when he was doubtful for England in the build-up to the 2002 World Cup after being hurt in European action for Manchester United. But Billy Bly got exactly the same injury in the autumn of 1947 while training at Boothferry Park when he slipped while skipping in the well below the best stand! He was taken to Hull Royal Infirmary for an X-ray, which showed that he had a broken bone, and it was initially thought that he would be out of action for a month - a fair bit less than the prognosis for Beckham. As it was, Bly was replaced by Peter Atkinson and then Hannaby for seven League games and a cuptie before he returned in early December for an FA Cup first-round replay at Southport after having been sidelined for the more regulation two months.

Bly played in two cupties and four League games before 1948 began with another injury setback. During City's first match of the year - a 4-2 victory away to Accrington Stanley - Bly was hurt in a challenge also involving his teammate Wilf Hassall and ex-Tiger Dennis Smith and damaged his left wrist. It was later confirmed that Billy had this time been injured by one of his own colleagues because he explained: "Wilf fell on it as we were clearing from opposition forwards." Bly carried on, but his wrist soon became swollen and was bandaged up at the end of the game. An X-ray two days later indicated that the wrist was broken, so he was ruled out of the forthcoming FA Cup third-round tie at home to First Division Middlesbrough. Hannaby, by then on the transfer list with Atkinson, played in the cuptie, but soon afterwards he moved to Halifax Town. City already had one Scottish goalkeeper on their books, Willie Russell, and early in 1948 they signed another, Alec Corbett, who deputised in goal for the next six League games.

Bly returned towards the end of February for the 3-1 defeat at Hartlepools United and promptly got injured in it. He damaged an ankle and Corbett again had to replace him, this time for just two games. Bly was then back for the final 11 matches of another campaign in which injuries had deprived him of continuity and City had had to use four goalkeepers.

Raich Carter was the Tigers' player-manager by the 1948-49 season and it turned out to be a momentous promotion campaign as they won the Third Division North title. It was probably not insignficant that Billy Bly for once had a relatively injury-free season and, strangely enough, it was not until February 26, 1949 - when City lost 1-0 at home to holders Manchester United in the sixth round of the FA Cup in front of the highest gate ever at Boothferry Park of 55,019 - that disaster struck. He was initially thought to have fractured his jaw, but a visit to a specialist and an X-ray examination showed that that he had, in fact, broken both the right and left bones in his nose. It was another instance of damage being done to Billy by one of his own teammates because he later explained: "Our wing-half Jimmy Greenhalgh kicked out as I dived for the ball and my nose got in the way of his boot. For the remainder of the match I played with concussion, remembering nothing. After the interval I went to the wrong end and my teammates said that under normal conditions I would have saved United's winner."

The injury forced Bly out of the next three League games, in which he was replaced by Joe Robinson, a recent signing from Blackpool. But then he was back for the next four matches of City's promotion push before he was hurt in a 3-2 victory away to Chester on April 2. Ten minutes before halftime he received a facial injury in trying in vain to prevent Joe Davies from giving Chester the lead and had to go off with Willie Buchan taking over from him in goal. Buchan, in fact, had regularly been a goalkeeper at Grangemouth High School and had previously taken on the role in an emergency during his prewar spell with Glasgow Celtic. Bly, meanwhile, returned before halftime at Chester, but briefly went on to the right wing before resuming in goal for the second half. He was still forced to miss the next game at home to York City four days later because of a problem with his eye although it was also decided that he should not be risked because of the hectic run-in towards the end of the season. The Tigers lost 3-2 - one of only four League defeats that season - and Robinson, a North-Easterner himself because he originated from Ashington in Northumberland, again stood in for Bly, who was then able to return to action for the last nine games of the successful promotion charge.

Having missed only four League games in helping City to promotion, Billy produced an action replay when he tasted Second Division soccer for the first time in 1949-50. He played in the first 29 League games and four FA Cup ties before his growing injury jinx struck him down again. This time it was double trouble in a 1-0 defeat away to Grimsby Town on February 18, 1950, when he was left limping with a sprain in his right foot and a damaged shoulder. Bly had already been struck on the forehead by a pointblack shot from Stan Lloyd - Tom Berry also received a facial knock early on - but he was hobbling later in the game as he bravely played on and it was felt that he was handicapped in trying to keep out Billy Cairns' winner seven minutes from the end. Bly was immediately given heat treatment and an X-ray showed that he had a badly-bruised left shoulder although his ankle injury was not too serious. Robinson, though, still had to replace him until he returned for the final nine games of a season in which City finished seventh in the table.

If Billy had not suffered unduly with injury by his own standards for two seasons, then the 1950-51 campaign was to be disastrous in comparison. The Tigers dropped to 10th in the table, but Bly saw little of the action even though he started as the first-choice goalkeeper as usual. He played in only five League games and was left out after the first four, but the jinx struck with a vengeance when he was recalled at the injured Robinson's expense for a game at Chesterfield on October 14. The match ended in a goalless draw and the Tigers' trainer George Lax had to attend to a series of knocks to Hassall, Viggo Jensen, Harold Meens, Freddie Smith, who was later to become a Chesterfield player, and Alf Ackerman in addition to Bly. The biggest setback, though, was the injury to Bly in the 35th minute when he suffered a broken right arm and had to be rushed to Chesterfield Royal Hospital. Not surprisingly, he did not see the rest of the match and Don Revie, who had also had to take over from Robinson a week earlier when he was hurt in a 3-1 home defeat against Leicester City, had to deputise for him in goal. Ackerman spent much of the second half limping, so the Tigers did well to earn a draw. They stopped for a meal in Chesterfield afterwards and Bly, who was also visited by his opposite number in the game, Ray Middleton, was able to rejoin his teammates for it.

But his first match back had proved costly because it was thought from the outset that he would be absent for two months: as it was, he missed the rest of the Second Division action that season as Robinson again stood in for him although John Savage also had a brief run in the first team. Bly finally made his comeback in the reserves at Doncaster in April 1951 when there were only four League games left although he did play in first-team friendlies away to Scarborough and Peterborough United later in the month and he did turn out in three of the club's five end-of-season tour matches.

Billy later told of the difficult battle that he faced to re-establish himself and repair his confidence after the broken arm at Chesterfield had kept him out of action longer than any other injury: "One of the attackers lashed at the ball as I stuck out my hand to save and my arm fell loosely by my side. It was quite accidental, but it proved to be my most troublesome injury. By now it was not just a physical cause I had to fight because there was a natural mental reaction. On resuming training, the first shot I faced was a hard drive into a corner from big Harold Meens. I went across confidently to catch it with both hands. My right hand was but an inch from the ball, but then I suddenly pulled it away. It was something beyond my control - a quite involuntary movement. But the writing was on the wall and I immediately realised that it was something I had to master or I would probably never return again to top-line soccer. There was only one possible line of action and that was to go out and save shot after shot, proving to myself that I had no weakness. For two days I had colleagues shooting hour after hour at me until any sub-conscious doubt about my hand was finally cleared away."

The Tigers dropped to 18th in the Second Division in 1951-52, but Billy Bly was back in League harness for the start of the season and played in the first 27 League matches until his cup luck again ran out. He had already been forced to miss FA Cup ties against notable opposition such as Blackburn Rovers, Middlesbrough and Everton and had received his only injury of 1948-49 in the quarter-finals against Manchester United. Three seasons later City had the opportunity of vengeance in the third round against United, but Bly's ever-present sequence in 1951-52 ended when he was injured the week before the cuptie. On January 5, 1952, the Tigers trounced Coventry City 5-0 at home and Bly damaged his shoulder in the first half. He later had a precautionary X-ray, which indicated that there was a sprained ligament rather than a break, so he was given a course of special heat treatment and hopes were high that they would be fit to go to Old Trafford for the cuptie. Bly even stayed behind for treatment while the rest of City's players enjoyed a day's golf at Bridlington as a break from training, but in the end he was ruled out of the revenge mission when United were sensationally beaten 2-0. Furthermore, Bly missed the fourth-round defeat at Blackburn and the next five League matches.

He then returned in place of Robinson for a 3-2 home win over Leeds United and played in a run of five League games before he was again in the wars. The struggling Tigers began their Easter programme with a 5-0 defeat at Everton on Good Friday and the following day they lost 4-0 at Nottingham Forest, a game in which Viggo Jensen was controversially sent off and Bly badly bruised his ribs. The injury forced him to miss the return game at home to Everton on Easter Monday and the final two games of the season as Robinson again stepped in.

For the third time in six postwar years Bly missed the end of a season because of injury, but he had always been in situ at the start of each campaign. That, though, changed in 1952. After missing the last three matches of the previous season with a rib injury, he missed the first 11 games of the next one with the same kind of problem. He suffered a bruised chest in the final pre-season practice match in readiness for 1952-53 and Robinson retained his place in the side until a 5-1 defeat at Barnsley. Bly then came in for eight games, making his comeback against a Fulham side whose youngest forward had been in prolific goalscoring form - Bobby Robson.

After beating Fulham in the first League meeting between the clubs for 17 years, City lost seven games in a row with Bly in goal. The Tigers' troubles were mounting because their experienced former England defender Neil Franklin was struggling with a knee problem and they had been refused permission to play one of Jensen's Danish compatriots, Jens Peter Hansen. Bly then reported unfit after having had to have a whitlow lanced, Robinson was recalled and City beat Notts County 6-0 at home. They then lost 5-0 away to Leicester City, but Robinson played in a run of nine League games and two FA Cup ties.

Bly was recalled for the return clash at home to Barnsley and played in a sequence of eight

League matches before he was again on Easter injury parade in 1953. He took a slight knock on his right ankle in the 2-1 defeat away to Lincoln City on Good Friday, but played in the 2-0 victory at home to Birmingham City the next day when he promptly aggravated the injury. It was sufficient to interfere with Bly's ability to kick properly, so Robinson stood in for the return meeting with Lincoln on Easter Monday. Bly, though, was back for the final five games of another disappointing campaign in which the Tigers again finished in 18th spot.

Robinson moved into non-League soccer to take over as player-manager of Wisbech Town during the summer of 1953 and Billy Bly, as ever, remained City's first-choice goalkeeper with Tommy Forgan, who had been at Boothferry Park since 1949 without having played for the first team, as his accepted deputy. Bly played in the opening eight games of the 1953-54 season before Forgan, who was himself from the North-East because he had been born in Middlesbrough, finally got some first-team action in the League. There was a double irony because he had, in fact, played a senior game the previous March - against the Tigers for Djurgarden in an emergency in a floodlit friendly at Boothferry Park - and he had missed most of 1953-54 because of injury! He had had a broken toe, but Bly had damaged his arm in diving at Tommy Briggs' feet in a 2-0 home defeat against Blackburn Rovers in which Tom Berry and Brian Bulless were also injured, so Forgan was given his League debut, retaining his place for five games.

Bly returned in mid-October and played in the next 18 League games, but there was a problem towards the end of the 14th one in the sequence. Again Blackburn were involved and again it was cuptie time. City played Rovers in the Second Division on January 23, 1954, and lost 3-1 in what was a precursor to a meeting between the two sides in the fourth round of the FA Cup at Ewood Park a week later. There was a hectic finish with two goals and an accidental collision in which Bly broke his nose in the time added on for stoppages. Syd Gerrie took over in goal for the last moments of the game and Bly was taken to hospital in Blackburn for an X-ray before rejoining his colleagues for the homeward journey to Hull, where he immediately received further treatment. But he was ruled out of the cuptie although he was back in action immediately afterwards after it had ended in a 2-2 draw and Forgan had taken his place.

But Bly soon sustained the most cruel and controversial injury of the many that bedevilled him during his lengthy career. City had played a number of friendly games since the installation of floodlights at Boothferry Park and on March 8, 1954, they were scheduled to entertain Scottish side Falkirk. He had let in eight goals in a game against them for Hamilton Academicals during the War years and they again proved to be one of his bogey's sides - for a different reason.

Bly had been reluctant to play in the friendly because he had been called up as a travelling reserve with the England B squad for a representative game against their counterparts from West Germany in Gelsenkirchen. It was the first international representative game between the two countries since the War and, on a personal note, it was due reward for the consistency that Bly had shown with the Tigers throughout many seasons. Sheffield United's Ted Burgin was the first-choice goalkeeper, but the England B party also included two of Manchester United's famed Busby Babes, Roger Byrne and Duncan Edwards, Bly's former City teammate Don Revie and Fulham hero Johnny Haynes.

As a friendly, City's game with Falkirk, which took place before the international, might have been a suitable occasion on which to give one of Bly's understudies a little more experience, but manager Bob Jackson insisted that he should play. He made enforced changes on the wings with Charlie Atkinson and Brian Cripsey replacing Johnny Stephens and Brian

Bulless, who had been hurt two days earlier in a 2-2 draw away to Plymouth Argyle, in which Bly had been ruled to have fouled Peter Langman in giving away a penalty. Bly had ruefully insisted later: "I was in the next parish!" By the Monday evening he wished that he had been.

The Tigers won the friendly against Falkirk 7-1, but Bly, Frank Harrison and Alf Ackerman were all added to an injury list that already included Ken Harrison, Stephens and Bulless. Jackson reflected: "It is just one of those things which run in cycles." But the hurt was to go far deeper for Billy Bly.

Early in the game Bly damaged his elbow when Falkirk's centre-forward Angus Plumb ran into him as he fisted the ball to safety. But then in the 20th minute Bly trapped his left arm between the ball and the crossbar as he attempted a save and he fell awkwardly. A bone in his left wrist had been broken and his chance of representative honours had gone. Trevor Porteous, who had ironically been doubtful for the friendly after having picked up a knee injury at Plymouth, replaced Bly in goal for 10 minutes while Forgan got changed and was allowed to come on as a substitute.

Bly's hopes of representative honours had disappeared as he faced the prospect of his forearm being in plaster for at least a month. And he reflected: "I don't think I will be able to play again this season and my inability to accept my call-up is the biggest disappointment that I have ever had. I would have liked to go to Germany because I played so many games on the Continent with the Combined Services team and to return would have revived old memories. It was the nearest I had got to an FA honour, but the hoodoo was around. Sir Stanley Rous has twice told me: 'If you keep on playing as you have been doing, you will be getting honours one of these days.' The first occasion was in Germany in 1945 and the other was at Tottenham when City played a League game there in 1949-50. Nothing has ever come of it until now. It is the first time in 17 years that representative honours have come my way and I hope that I will get another chance despite my present misfortune."

Bly was indeed forced to miss the final 11 games of the season as Forgan and then David Teece deputised and the repercussions of his disappointment about missing the international call-up were felt throughout the family because his wife, Dorothy, said: "He would loved to have played. Perhaps he might have gone on to greater things if he'd played." It was not quite the end of the story, though, because City then added insult to Bly's injury.

Roy Bly explained: "City were told that they were playing a friendly game and the players had to do as they were told. My dad was told: 'You're playing.' And he had to play. But he made the point that he had more to lose if he got injured. Being prone to injury, he was more than concerned that he had been made to play because he was going to represent his country.

"I think everybody would feel the same, but Bob Jackson made him play and just before halftime he jumped up high for the ball in typical fashion. But having brittle bones, he snapped his wrist against the crossbar. In those days I think he got £3 for a friendly game, but, when he went in at halftime, Bob Jackson handed him half the amount - 30 shillings to him - because he had played in less than only half a game. My dad nearly dragged Bob Jackson up to see the chairman, Harold Needler. It was one of the few times that I heard about him losing his temper. In fact, he told Mr. Needler that he thought that it was an absolute disgrace. But the footballer in those days was like any other working man. There were no big wages or spin-offs. The commercial world hadn't come into football then."

In the summer of 1954 Forgan moved to York City, whom he helped to the semi-finals of the FA Cup while they were only a Third Division North side, and Bly was back in harness for the

Tigers by the beginning of the following season, but it was to be another stop-start saga for him. This time there were to be two more injury lay-offs during the course of the 1954-55 campaign. Bly played in 27 of the League games, but the side slumped to 19th in the table by the end of the season.

Bly was in goal for the first five games, four of which they had won after losing 2-0 away to Leeds United on the opening day. In the fifth match on September 4, 1954, Bob Crosbie scored all of City's goals in a 4-2 triumph at home to Ipswich Town, but Bly damaged his heel during it and had to pull out of the visit to West Ham United two days later. An SOS was sent to Teece to travel to London by train with the City party after Bly, who had thought that he would be fit, had telephoned the club to withdraw. He missed four games, only one of which was won, and returned towards the end of September, playing in the next eight matches before Teece regained his place after City, who were again engaged in a series of floodlit friendlies at Boothferry Park, had beaten a side called the Starlights 7-1.

Bly was back in Tigers' first team for the FA Cup in January, 1955, playing in a 2-0 defeat at home to Birmingham City in the third round. He then appeared in nine consecutive League games before yet another Easter injury setback occurred. On April 2 Bly was hurt as he did well in a 1-0 defeat at Bristol Rovers, for whom goalkeeper Howard Radford ironically lost his ever-present playing record for the season because of injury. Bly made several daring saves and on one occasion he badly damaged his wrist when diving at the feet of Alfie Biggs. The injury did not turn out to be as bad as was first feared, but it was still enough to keep him out of the Tigers' three-match Easter programme - against Bury twice and, almost predictably, Blackburn. Teece deputised in the first two games, the powerfully-built Ron Capewell made his only first-team appearance for City in the return meeting with Bury at Boothferry Park on Easter Monday, keeping a clean sheet, and yet Bly returned for the final five matches of the season.

City, who had replaced manager Bob Jackson with Bob Brocklebank, were to be relegated from the Second Division in 1955-56 and the season began badly for the team as a whole and Billy Bly as an individual. The Tigers lost 12 out of their first 15 League games, winning only once in that time, and Bly was in and out of the side because of injuries. He played in the first two matches, the latter of which was a 2-0 defeat away to Lincoln City that produced a lengthy casualty list for the Tigers. Tom Berry and Syd Gerrie recovered from knocks in time to visit Liverpool at Anfield for the third game of the season, but Bly, Brian Bulless and Viggo Jensen were all ruled out. In Bly's case an X-ray showed that he had cracked a bone in an ankle and he was missing for four games while Teece took over in goal.

Bly returned for five more games, in which struggling City conceded a total of 16 goals. The last match in the sequence was a 5-0 defeat at Fulham and the Tigers' injury problems again struck them with a vengeance. George Patterson had to pull out because he was found to have a leg infection on the night before the game so that City were unable to name an unchanged side for the first time that season, Berry was off the field to have attention to a pulled muscle when the prolific Bedford Jezzard scored Fulham's second goal and Bly fell awkwardly shortly before halftime and further damaged the troublesome ankle that he had first injured at Lincoln. Teece replaced him for the next match, which turned out to be his last in the first team for City, because Bernard Fisher and Barry Lord were both injured, too. But then Fisher, who had not yet turned professional, was given his League debut after being brought in for a floodlit friendly against top Hungarian side Vasas and played in three games, in which he let in 11 goals, before Bly returned for a long spell in the side.

Bly appeared in the next 19 League games and two FA Cup ties as City's form improved a little, but they still began to look doomed and eventually it was Easter, Blackburn and, uncannily, injury time once more for him. On Good Friday, 1956, Bly was hurt in a 2-0 defeat at Blackburn and was forced to miss the final eight games of the season when it was discovered that he had broken his ankle. It also caused a poser for 22-year-old Fisher because he was due to get married at 10am on Easter Saturday! Fisher, therefore, had to leave his wedding reception in his home city of York to dash to Boothferry Park and play in a 2-2 draw against Fulham. This particular honeymoon period lasted for the return meeting at home to Blackburn on Easter Monday and the remaining six games of the season, but the biggest irony of it all was that on Easter Saturday Fisher had originally - and conveniently - been destined to play in a Midland League match for City Reserves against York at nearby Bootham Crescent before Bly was injured!

City were back in the old Third Division North for the 1956-57 season and Bly was back in goal for most of it. He played in the first nine League matches, but was then ruled out for the next six after being hurt in a 1-0 defeat at Derby County on September 15, 1956. The Rams bombarded City with crosses early in the game and Bly fell awkwardly when he moved out to try to intercept one. He twisted his ankle, but managed to limp through the rest of the game and gave a typically-gritty performance in the face of his adversity. The ankle was not broken and an initial X-ray suggested that Bly might be suffering from a sprain, but a damaged ligament was later diagnosed. It was still sufficient to keep him out of the trip to Bradford Park Avenue two days later when City were forced to make five changes overall and Bly's injury caused a particular problem. Fisher was on National Service and his release from his Army unit could not be obtained, so Mauno Rintanen, a Finnish international, deputised in goal as he and left-back Ken Smales made their debuts for the Tigers. Rintanen, an amateur who had business commitments in England, played in three successive games, Fisher came in for the next two, Rintanen made his fourth and final appearance for the club and then Bly returned in mid-October for the rest of the season. City finished seventh in the Third Division North and were unbeaten at home in the league from September 22, while Bly had a comparatively injury-free season and played in 43 out of 49 games overall.

City moved up three places in the table in 1957-58, but what seemed to be the natural order for Bly was restored because he was forced on to the sidelines with injuries on three separate occasions. Bly damaged his ribs in the second game of the season at home to Barrow, so Len Round, a close-season signing from Ayr United, was quickly given his debut for the club. Round, an Englishman who had served in the Royal Scots Fusiliers, played in the next nine games before Bly was restored to the first team at the end of September, 1957.

But it was a short stay because Bly was again injured after his third match back when City won 1-0 away to Carlisle United. This time he fell on the Boothferry Park terracing during training two days before the next game at home to Bury and was ruled out for the next four matches. Manager Bob Brocklebank had already named an unchanged side for the clash with high-riding Bury when Bly limped into the dressing-room. He had gone out on to the concrete steps that were used for what was known as the Tigers' "wind and legs" training up and down the terraces. But he stubbed his toe on one step and then hit his knee on the next one. He had four stitches inserted immediately in his gashed knee and was then sent for an X-ray after it had stiffened up overnight, but he had to face another lay-off and Round again had to deputise.

Bly was back in first-team action for City by mid-November and played in three FA Cup ties and two League games before he was injured again. On December 9 the Tigers beat Port Vale

4-3 in an FA Cup second-round replay at Boothferry Park that went into extra time and it took its toll. Bly, Andy Davidson and Paul Feasey were injured and Norman Neilson, Bill Bradbury and Brian Bulless went down with colds before the next League game at home to Southport. As it was, Bly, who had unusally been deemed as a possible candidate to be dropped in favour of Round for the first cuptie with Vale, was the only one who did not make it. He was kicked on his foot during a goalmouth scramble in the closing stages of the cup replay and was hardly able to stand on it although he managed to cycle to Boothferry Park two days later for treatment under a heat-ray lamp. Bly still had to miss nine games, Round standing in for him for the first four of them and Fisher taking over for the next five, which included two more cupties. Bly returned for the Tigers' sixth and final cuptie of the season - a 4-3 defeat at Sheffield Wednesday in the fourth round - and then played in the remaining 19 League matches, but it had been another campaign that had lacked continuity because of his injury woes.

Billy Bly's recurring injury problems meant that he was never to play in every game for City in any season, but he was close to doing so during 1958-59 and it was another promotion triumph. Bly played in 45 out of the 46 League games and their only FA Cup tie - a depressing 1-0 defeat at home to Stockport County. The Third Division had transcended the more regional Third Division North and the Tigers had an exemplary home record in the League, losing only once to Newport County during the season on October 4, 1958. Perhaps significantly, it was the one match in which Bly was injured, which was hardly surprising because it was a robust encounter in which Newport won 3-2 on their first visit to Boothferry Park. City had a home game against Chesterfield, whom Brocklebank had once managed, two days after it and Bly and Denis Durham were missing because of injury and Frank Harrison was omitted after he had asked for a transfer because of the barracking that he had been receiving from the fans. It meant that there were League debuts for Barry Lord, Bly's replacement, and Graham Wilkinson. Bly had suffered double trouble against Newport because he had been knocked out after receiving a kick on the back of the neck and he had pulled a thigh muscle, which had prevented him from taking goal-kicks for much of the game. Lord, then a well-built 20-year-old, was from Goole, but he had only one first-team outing on this occasion because Bly returned for a League game at Stockport the following Saturday and kept his place in the promotion side, who finished as runners-up to Plymouth Argyle, for the rest of the season.

At the age of 39 Billy Bly was back in the old Second Division. It was to be his last season with the Tigers and typically he had some injury setbacks before his career with the club ended in acrimonious circumstances. Bly played in half of the League games - 21 - and City's only FA Cup tie - another 5-0 defeat at Fulham - but he was injured after only two League games.

After the newly-promoted Tigers had started with a 3-1 home win over newly-promoted Plymouth, they were thrashed 6-0 away to Sheffield United two days later and then Bly was injured in training a further three days afterwards before the third game of the season against Liverpool at Anfield. He pulled up during a sprinting session at Boothferry Park and complained about a pain in his thigh, so he was immediately sent for two treatment sessions. But Bly was diagnosed as having a strained thigh muscle and Fisher took his place for the 5-3 defeat against Liverpool in front of a crowd of 35,520, the highest for a match involving the Tigers that season.

City continued to leak goals, but Fisher kept his place for seven matches until Bly returned for a 1-0 defeat away to Rotherham United in late September. He had a nine-match run in the side until his injury hoodoo struck again during a 3-1 win at home to Brighton and Hove

Albion. Towards the end of the game he suffered a strained thigh muscle for the second time that season and, although it responded to treatment because he had not had to play on with it for very long, he still needed a fitness test before City's visit to Stoke City the following Saturday. It took place shortly before City set off for their overnight headquarters at Buxton, but Bly was ruled out for the next two games when Lord again stood in for him because Fisher was also out of commission - because of a stomach-muscle strain.

Bly returned for a 3-1 victory at Sunderland when Dave King scored twice for the Tigers on his League debut and played in seven consecutive League games and the cuptie at Fulham. But then he damaged his back in a 1-1 draw against Bristol City at Boothferry Park on January 23, 1960, and was left out of a friendly at home to Leeds United the following Saturday. Lord replaced Bly as a precautionary measure for a game which Leeds, who had also been knocked out of the FA Cup in the third round, won 1-0 with a goal by Jack Charlton and stayed in for the next League fixture. Fisher then took over for four League matches as Bly's back trouble failed to clear up, but it was at least the last injury that was to plague him in City's colours. He recovered from it to play three more League games before he missed the rest of the 1959-60 season as the Tigers prepared to give him a free transfer and sever his links with the club.

Bly's injuries with Hull City forced him to miss many games and he would have been much closer to Andy Davidson's record number of League appearances for the club without all the enforced absences. In addition, there were several occasions when Bly received knocks, but gallantly played on without having to be out of action.

During one week in September 1947, for example, Bly was injured in the closing stages of an away game against Rotherham United when he was left dazed after a collision with their prolific marksman Wally Ardron. In fact, he had somehow managed to cling on to the ball as he lay on the ground. There then followed a midweek home defeat against Halifax Town and two days later Bly appeared at Stockport County for another goalless draw "wearing a plaster above his right eye to cover scars of an injury sustained on Thursday night."

Bly also had to battle on in pain during the record-breaking start to the 1948-49 title-winning season when he picked up two knocks in the 3-0 home win over Wrexham. He was left hobbling after damaging his right thigh in a collision with Wrexham's centre-forward Dick Yates early in the second half and was then shaken up in the 65th minute when he tried to prevent another forward, Fred Rowell, from scoring, but he managed to soldier on.

On the final day of 1955 Bly ricked his ankle in a 1-1 draw away to Plymouth Argyle and that made him doubtful for the third round of the FA Cup a week later. But City had been drawn at Aston Villa, who were struggling in the First Division, and Bly was determined to play. The injury was strapped up, but he managed only one goal-kick before full-backs John Neal, later a Villa player, and Viggo Jensen had to take over from him. The Tigers still managed a 1-1 draw - they lost the replay 2-1 at Boothferry Park - even though Bly admitted: "I could feel the pain shooting through my ankle." But he battled on in front of 32,865 fans and it was reported: "Hull City's Billy Bly must take the biscuit for sheer guts and bravery." It was further noted: "The whole City side had to fall back in defence for long spells, but Villa had no success because many of their shots were off the mark and those that were accurate were brilliantly dealt with by Bly."

The replay, which the Tigers lost 2-1, was described as "one of the roughest, toughest games Boothferry Park has seen" and Bly's legacy was a cut lip. The League game at home to Stoke City two days later did not take place, but Bly was still scheduled to take his place in the team as he, Andy Davidson and Bill Bradbury all looked ready to shake off knocks that they had received in the replay.

Bly also showed his courage in the early part of the 1958-59 promotion season. The Tigers drew 0-0 at home to Swindon Town on September 1, 1958, and in the 25th minute Bly bravely came out to whisk the ball off the toes of opposing centre-forward Alec Moyse. But he had to go off for six minutes for some stitches to his left eye after they had collided and Bill Bradbury took over temporarily in goal. Bly returned with a bandage round his head and would presumably have been nicknamed Rambo nowadays: former England forward Len Shackleton was reporting on the match then, though, and insisted that he resembled an Eastern prince, labelling him Abdul! But Shackleton was quick to praise his fortitude and wrote: "'Abdul' Bly had the crowd on their toes with three super saves, two of them from outside-left Arnold d'Arcy, both spanking shots from just inside the box and worthy of goals."

Roy Bly can remember one whimsical incident from Billy's playing days when he started to understand about football injuries. Nowadays players get the best treatment as possible as soon as possible in a more pampered atmosphere although there is nothing wrong with that: it was different in Billy Bly's day, though. Jimmy Lodge, a former City player who had at one time also played for the club under the name of Barrass, was the physiotherapist at Boothferry Park for a long time from the ground's opening. Naturally it meant that he got to know Billy very well! Like Billy, he originated from the North-East and Roy recalled: "When we still had a shop near Booth-ferry Park, I went down to the ground with my dad when he was calling in for some treatment and I met Jimmy Lodge, who was a character. He had a cigarette stuck to his top lip and every other word he used was a swear word. All he had to use were a leather bench, a heat lamp, a shelf with three brown bottles on it and his hands! I thought to myself: 'No wonder dad spent so long being injured because it would be such a slow process getting him fit again.'"

Injuries always haunted Billy, however. When he joined Weymouth during the 1961-62 season after Hull City had released him, he stayed reasonably injury-free although he did break a finger. As Weymouth built up to their crucial FA Cup fourth-round tie away to Preston North End, player-manager Frank O'Farrell confided: "Billy has been playing for four weeks with the broken finger, but now it is healing itself. He really is a marvel." But Roy Bly insisted anyway: "Broken fingers never worried my dad. He always said that he got over them by taping two of them together."

But there must have been something in the East Yorkshire air that affected him adversely. He rejoined Hull Brunswick, then playing in the Second Division of the Yorkshire League, for 1962-63 and was promptly injured. On August 25, 1962, he played for them in a 1-1 draw away to Ossett Town and broke his right arm. He initially got a kick when diving for the ball and then aggravated the knock when he clashed with an opponent while jumping for it. It meant that he had difficulty in picking the ball up, so he went off two minutes before halftime, left-winger Alan Beatham becoming the latest in the conveyor-belt of outfield players to deputise for him in goal. Billy was taken by ambulance to hospital in Wakefield, where a temporary plaster was put on the arm, and later had further treatment at Hull Royal Infirmary. Despite having had another date with a plaster cast, he scoffed at the idea that he ought to retire from playing at the age of 42: "Give up? Why should I? I'm still enjoying my game, so why worry? It's not killing me."

The injuries still stalked Billy, though. When he went to work at what was then Everthorpe Borstal in the 1970s, he was persuaded to play in a Thompson Cup tie for prison staffs from all

A happy family - Billy (right) with (left to right) his father
William, wife Dorothy and mother Annie in the summer of 1954.

Billy's wife Dorothy.

Billy and Dorothy's children Norma
and Roy.

Billy and Norma indulge in a spot of light reading.

Billy helps Roy to try on his first
slipper - a present from Hull City's
1950 tour of Turkey.

Billy and Dorothy relax in later
years.

Billy lines up for a wartime photograph with the BAOR team. As usual, he could not resist the temptation to collect the requisite autographs.

Billy (back row, third from the left) in uniform with his Army colleagues at Hamburg in May 1946.

Billy (left) lines up for the National Anthem before a wartime match in Antwerp alongside England international full-back Eddie Hapgood.

Billy the goalkeeper poses at regimental headquarters shortly before demobilisation in 1946.

Hull City in 1938-39 (left to right): back row, Davies, Annables, Treanor, Riches, Meens, Stokes, Hardy, White, Woodhead; middle row, Robinson, Huxford, Trench, Ellis, Bly, Darling, Dickinson, Salvidge, Jimmy Lodge (assistant trainer); front row, Ernest Blackburn (secretary-manager), Lawrence, McNeill, Blyth, Sullivan, Duffy, Cunliffe, Sherwood, Hubbard, Joe Beck (trainer).

Billy lines up for Hull City just before the aborted 1939-40 season. Pictured (left to right) are: back row, Clubley, Self, Meens, Jimmy Lodge (assistant trainer), Rodger, Clarke, Hall; middle row, J.Robinson, Riches, Gilmore, Bly, Curnow, Watson, Woods, Smith; front row, Ernest Blackburn (secretary-manager), Richardson, Prescott, Cunliffe, C.Robinson, Davis, Woodhead, Joe Beck (trainer); on the ground, Kavanagh, Lowe.

Hull City's Third Division North title-winning squad of 1948-49 (left to right): back row, M.Craddock, J.Wright, J.Taylor, W.Buchan, N.Moore, F.Seddon; middle row, W.Hassall, G.King, H.Meens, A.Corbett, T.Berry, W.Bly, D.Durham, N.Fowler, G.Bradshaw; front row, Jimmy Lodge (physiotherapist), J.Bloomer, A.Conway, Kenneth Percival (president), H.Carter, Harold Needler (chairman), J.Greenhalgh, E.Burbanks, George Lax (trainer); on the ground, K.Harrison, A.Mellor.

A group of Hull City players relax before the club's FA Cup giant-killing episode at Grimsby Town in January 1949. They are (left to right): Jack Taylor, Norman Fowler, Willie Buchan (seated), Jimmy Greenhalgh, Viggo Jensen, Ken Harrison, Allan Mellor, Billy Bly, Harold Meens, Jimmy Bloomer, Raich Carter, Tom Berry.   [Grimsby Evening Telegraph]

Hull City in 1953-54 (left to right): back row, Frank Harrison, Bill Harris, Tom Berry, Billy Bly, Denis Durham, Viggo Jensen; front row, Ken Harrison, Ken Horton, Syd Gerrie, Alf Ackerman, Brian Bulless. [Provincial]

Hull City in 1956-57 (left to right): back row, Les Collinson, Frank Harrison, Paul Feasey, Billy Bly, Denis Durham, Andy Davidson; front row, Johnny Stephens, Doug Clarke, Bill Bradbury, Brian Bulless, Brian Cripsey. [Provincial]

Hull City in 1959-60 (left to right): back row, Mike Brown, Paul Feasey, Brian Garvey, Andy Davidson, Billy Bly, Brian Bulless, Les Collinson, Angus McLean (coach); front row, Doug Clarke, Roy Shiner, Jackie Sewell, Ralph Gubbins, Bill Bradbury.   [A.Wilkes and Son]

The Blazer Boys - Billy (centre) lines up with long-standing teammates Andy Davidson (left) and Denis Durham.

Hull City on their end-of-season visit to Turkey in May 1950. Billy is sixth from the left on the back row.

The Hull City party line up soon after their arrival in Spain for their end-of-season tour in May 1951. Billy is in the centre at the back.

The Hull City Association Football Club Company, Limited

(Incorporated 1946)

Members of the Football Association; Football League; Midland League.

President: Kenneth Percival

Secretary Manager:
Major FRANK C. BUCKLEY

Telephone Central 32872

Directors:
Kenneth Percival
Harold Needler *(Chairman)*
G. H. Needler
John Needler
F. R. Metcalfe
R. E. Buttery
W. R. Smith
G. T. Rignall
S. T. Kershaw

Telegrams: "TIGERS," HULL

Registered Office and Ground,

BOOTHFERRY PARK,

HULL.

Billy Bly always liked to collect the autographs of his teammates. In this instance he used headed Hull City notepaper to get those of the 1947-48 squad.

HULL CITY
FIXTURES 1950-51

Sigma Signs Ltd., 222 Spring Bank, Hull

BILLY BLY

(Hull City A.F.C. Goalkeeper)

Master Painter and Decorator

GENERAL

DECORATING

60 WORCESTER ROAD, HULL

Telephone 34179 (9 a.m. to 5 p.m.)

Billy Bly uses Hull City's 1950-51 fixture list to advertise his talents.

A group of Hull City players receive their benefit cheques from club officials in 1952-53 (left to right): Denis Durham, Harold Meens, president Kenneth Percival, chairman Harold Needler, Billy Bly, Tom Berry, Ken Harrison.

Billy contemplates the possibility of turning his hand to bowls.

Billy sports a broken nose after being hurt against Blackburn Rovers in January 1954.

Billy rests his broken arm as he and Ken Harrison relax on the Boothferry Park terracing.

Billy and fellow goalkeeper Joe Robinson pass the medicine ball in training during the 1948-49 season.

Billy makes the most of some spartan training facilities on the Boothferry Park car-park.

Billy uses a punch ball to help his training during the 1953-54 season.

Billy at full stretch in training.

Billy shows his courage in a 4-2 win at Halifax during Hull City's record start to the 1948-49 season.

Billy collects a cross in a goalless draw at Southport in April 1949.
[Provincial]

Billy demonstrates his bravery during Hull City's 3-2 giant-killing act in the FA Cup fourth round against Grimsby Town at Blundell Park in January 1949. [Grimsby Evening Telegraph]

Billy safely gathers the ball in at Grimsby in January 1949. [Grimsby Evening Telegraph]

Billy to the rescue in Hull City's 1-0 home win over Leeds United in October 1949.

One of Billy's finest hours - he competes with Tottenham Hotspur's Les Bennett at White Hart Lane in front of a **66,889** crowd in April 1950. [Keystone]

Billy agrees a deal to join Weymouth with their player-manager Frank O'Farrell at King's Cross railway station in November 1961.

Roy Bly runs out as Weymouth's mascot against Newport County in the FA Cup in November 1961.

Goalkeeper Billy and mascot Roy prepare for FA Cup action with Weymouth. (W. Anderson)

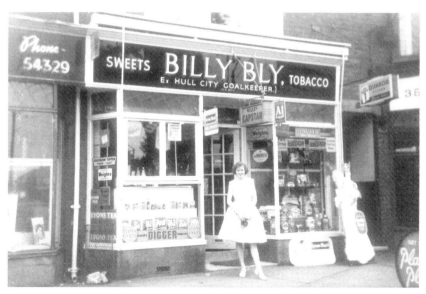

Norma poses outside Billy's famed sweet shop near Boothferry Park.

Former Hull City forward Brian Marwood (left) presents the Billy Bly Memorial Trophy to skipper David Norton in 1992 after the Tigers had beaten North Ferriby United 1-0 in their annual match. Marwood had been in digs with Billy and Dorothy Bly during his early years at Boothferry Park.

over the country. Everthorpe were playing Durham Jail and he broke his ankle.

Ex-Tiger Dave Fraser, a teammate that day, recalled: "Bill went up to catch a ball at crossbar height, came down on one ankle and broke it. He had to have a pin put into it and he spent many weeks recovering." Roy Bly also played in that game and has a rather more stark recollection of it because he said: "I remember helping out because they were short. My dad was in goal and we played a team from the North-East at Everthorpe. It was really physical and this guy went through my dad. He didn't care, but my dad had to have a pin put into his ankle. And that was the last game in which my father played.

"I've never known anybody like him for injuries and bad luck. He still enjoyed the odd game for the ex-Tigers or whoever. But here he was in his retirement after professional football and he still got crocked. But afterwards my dad just said: 'Oh, it's all right. It doesn't matter.' I think people do get over that kind of thing after a while when they're used to it. They know they have to get over it and to my dad an injury just seemed to be something that happened to him nearly every other day.

"He always used to play down his injuries. He'd say: 'That'll be all right' or 'That's nothing.' He never used to complain. He might have been on crutches and have a broken arm, an eye closed and a broken nose, but his attitude would be: 'I'm all right. It's nothing. I'll get over it.' It was as if he expected it because injuries happened so regularly. He didn't make much comment about them and tended to shrug them off. In later years he had a bit of arthritis in his joints and he used to feel it in his knees when going upstairs. But he remained reasonably fit into his late 40s."

Billy himself remained phlegmatic about his injury lay-offs even though he felt a certain amount of stigma attached to them. He said in an interview with the Yorkshire Evening Post in January 1957: "They call me soccer's most injured player and it is a title I'm not particularly proud of. I would be quite pleased to get rid of it, but claimants will have to go a bit. I reckon it is about time that a plaster of Paris firm put me on commission! My proneness to injury has worried me considerably and at one time I thought that I might just have extra-brittle bones, but all the doctors I have seen tell me that this is not so. It is not the fault of opposing forwards either. It is just that I put everything I have into the effort when I leave my line to challenge for the ball. I suppose the centre-forwards do the same and something has got to go - usually one of my bones - because I am only a lightweight and even now I scarcely tip the scales at 10 stones wet through. But I have no grumbles about the laws of the game as they stand despite all the knocks and not for one moment do I advocate that we should adopt the Continental practice of never allowing a goalkeeper to be charged in possession. A 50-50 chance is all I ask for, but I would like to see referees being stricter on players who obstruct goalkeepers at corners and giving us more protection when we are jumping at full stretch to gather high centres with our eyes on the ball."

And on another occasion Billy summed up his injury setbacks with a typically down-to-earth, professional approach: "They say that all goalkeepers are daft, but it's not much use standing on the goal-line and hoping for the best when you see a forward charging through." His wife, Dorothy, added: "He just went for the ball no matter what was in his way, but he nearly always came up with it. It was just his style and you would never have changed him. I suppose really that he was very lucky because all his breaks mended nicely..."

It is ironic and baffling as to why Billy Bly should have received so many injuries. They are part and parcel of football and there are always some players who seem to suffer more than most. Some have only occasional injuries and some have only mild, minor injuries, such as strains, pulls and bruises, but there are others whose injuries are customarily severe and regularly seem to end with a date with a plaster cast. In most cases they can end a career prematurely: in Billy Bly's case they just made him more determined than ever to bounce back time after time with relentless courage. And in Billy's case there was one reason why it was so mystifying that he should be beset by so many injury setbacks in the first place. After all, he regularly carried round a lucky rabbit's foot in his wallet. To that extent, it would appear that it brought Billy just about as much luck as it did the rabbit...

7

Happy Days

Only a handful of players have ever featured in two Hull City promotion campaigns and most of them played for the club in the 1980s. That was when the Tigers were promoted from the old Fourth Division in 1982-83 and the Third Division in 1984-85 with a near miss in-between. Garreth Roberts, one of only four players to have made more League appearances for City than Billy Bly, led both teams and nine others - Tony Norman, Gary Swann, Dennis Booth, Peter Skipper, Dale Roberts, Bobby McNeil, Andy Flounders, Billy Askew and Billy Whitehurst - also appeared in both campaigns.

City's other promotion seasons were more evenly spaced although the evergreen Andy David-son, one of the other four players to have made more League appearances for the club than Bly, Mick Milner and Les Collinson also appeared in two of them - in 1958-59 and 1965-66. But to play in two promotion campaigns 10 years apart takes some doing and shows some longevity, but that is just what Bly and Denis Durham achieved.

Bly, though, first had to establish himself as a first-team regular with the Tigers. He had first broken into a side who had plenty of potential and hopes were high that they would reclaim their place in the Second Division sooner rather than later, but the Second World War put a stop to their ambitions. Ernie Blackburn, the City manager who had signed Bly, had done well since taking over near the end of 1936. The side finished third, fifth and seventh in the Third Division North following the relegation season in 1935-36 and Bly had got his chance as an 18-year-old in the final eight official games before war broke out.

Jack Curnow, another goalkeeper from the North-East, played in the two games of the aborted 1939-40 season before hostilities began and turned out frequently for the Tigers during their wartime fixtures. But there were plenty of changes to herald a new outlook for City when organised League football returned for the 1946-47 season. Curnow, from Lingdale near Teesside, returned to Tranmere Rovers, Blackburn was not retained by the club's new board of directors and the Tigers moved to their new ground at Boothferry Park.

Bly played in half of City's League games in 1946-47 when they finished 11th in the Third Division North in the first season under Maj. Frank Buckley's management. Once they had settled down after failing to win any of their opening eight fixtures, they had a respectable defensive record and at one point Bly played in a run of seven games in which the Tigers conceded only three goals. But they used a high complement of players and finished four places lower than they had in the last previous full season under Blackburn in 1938-39.

Bly, though, made his mark in his first full season in League soccer and had a purple patch during the late autumn of 1946. It was reported after the Tigers had drawn 1-1 at Bradford City: "The backs and goalkeeper behaved magnificently and gradually wore down the home side, who were most enterprising in their shooting. Bly was applauded time and again for wonderful saves." A week later City drew 0-0 at Accrington Stanley and it was recorded: "Bly had a magnificent day in goal." When he returned from injury for an FA Cup tie at home to New Brighton, his performance was variously described as miraculous and masterly. And in the 2-1 win at Darlington in the second round it was said that "Bly was even more brilliant upon a further call" after he had saved from centre-forward Harry Clarke.

Bly was also in heroic form when the Tigers visited First Division Blackburn Rovers in the third round as they drew 1-1 before losing the replay 3-0 after he had been taken ill and missed out because of mumps. Watched by a big contingent of supporters, including Tom Hudson, of Hull Fishing Vessel Owners' Association, City fought for a famous draw in the first meeting and it was recorded: "Bly was cheered time and time again, but City's defence as a whole deserved the tumultuous applause given them at the conclusion of the struggle." Bly was at his best as Rovers pressed forward for a late winner - first with some "brilliant goalkeeping when he tipped the ball over from a smasher" from England international Bobby Langton and then when he "pulled off a wonder save by diving full-length near the post" from a free-kick. In addition, one Blackburn representative apparently even described Bly as being in the £15,000 class - the same as the famed England international goalkeeper Frank Swift!

In the second half of the season Bly was again at his best when City won 1-0 at Wrexham, who included England international and ex-Tiger Tommy Gardner, with a goal by Ron "Paddy" Brown. Wrexham had a good home record and it was noted: "Jimmy Greenhalgh, Billy Bly, Arthur Watson and James Mills were City's big quartet. Only once did Bly falter and that was when Gardner beat him to the ball to a side of City's goal. No damage was done, however, and, when Gardner looked a certain scorer later in the match, Bly did the seemingly impossible with a lightning advance to fall on the ball."

Buckley again employed a high number of players - 35 - in 1947-48 as he continued to experiment and struggled to field a settled side, but City were promotion contenders up to the end of January 1948. They then lost their way and went seven games without a win and the chance had gone. Bly, for his part, played in 27 League matches that season as the Tigers moved up to seventh in the table and further confirmed his talent.

It started on his return to action after injury in the first game of the season when City won 3-2 at Lincoln on August 23, 1947. He took a knock during the game, just as he had done against the Imps in the first fixture at Boothferry Park at the start of the previous season, but it was also noted: "City's defence were sound and Bly gave a good exhibition in goal. He was kept busy and responded well in the tense moments."

The rave notices continued throughout the season and Bly turned in a series of sparkling performances, many of them during the Tigers' seven matches in September 1947 when he also became a member of Chalk Lane Working-Men's Club in West Hull. He kept four clean sheets and conceded just four goals during the month. It was clear now that he was establishing his own reputation and endearing himself to the public in a way which was to stand him in good stead in later years.

City lost 1-0 away to Rochdale in the fourth game of the campaign on September 2, but national journalist Ivor Davies proclaimed: "It was Rochdale v. Bly at Spotland last night when Hull City suffered their first defeat. But for Bly's superb goalkeeping, the score might easily have been 10-0 without exaggeration of Rochdale's superiority. Bly was not beaten until the 70th minute, but the shots that did not beat him, numbering roughly 40, provoked a display of acrobatic and resolute goalkeeping that had an appreciative audience constantly cheering."

The following Saturday the Tigers drew 0-0 at Rotherham United, who were consistently one of the top sides in the Football League's lower divisions in those days. City lost skipper Jack Taylor with a torn calf muscle just before halftime and it was recorded: "The soccer was hard and gruelling and the players did not get away without some hard knocks. There were errors by both teams, but the defenders played a great game. It was a big afternoon for James Mills,

Harold Meens and Billy Bly, but City's team as a whole did well." Bly, almost naturally, took a heavy knock late on, but he was at his best at times: "When tremendous power was put behind a kick by Gladstone Guest, Bly came in for a great ovation as he pushed the ball wide for a corner. Bly's brilliance then got City out of another hot spot as the Rotherham forwards stormed the goal again."

A week later the Tigers drew 0-0 away to Stockport County and it was reported: "It was only the brilliance of Bly, in the Hull goal, that saved the Yorkshire side from defeat. He played a storming game and had much to do with City's defence holding all attacks."

On September 20 the Tigers beat Bradford City 2-1 at Boothferry Park in a game watched by Lord Calverley, who had helped them with the move to their new ground. City's goals came from Norman Moore and Len Robertson, who scored on his final League appearance for the club after being drafted in as a late replacement for Denis Durham. But George Murphy, who moved to City later in the season, was repeatedly denied by some excellent goalkeeping and it was also noted: "Bly was at his best again and more than once thwarted the visiting forwards."

A week later City won 2-0 at Barrow with goals by George Richardson and Moore, but it was pointed out: "Suffering their third successive home defeat, Barrow were largely beaten by Bly, the Hull City goalkeeper, who gave one of the finest displays of goalkeeping seen on the ground." Another report insisted: "Bly, in the City goal, was in brilliant form."

Bly returned for the FA Cup first round against their Third Division North rivals Southport after injury and was a hero in their 3-2 win in a replay after a 1-1 draw at Boothferry Park. One report indicated: "Southport went down fighting at Haig Avenue, but they were chiefly foiled by Bly, who resumed duty in the City goal after two months' absence because of a foot injury. He made many brilliant saves, especially from Andy Powell and Cecil Wyles, both of whom would have put their side on terms if the 'keeper had not been at his best." A further report stated: "Brilliant goalkeeping by Bly when Southport were all out for the equaliser was a major factor in his team's success." And the famed Desmond Hackett wrote: "Wyles swept in a perfect shot to beat Bly for the second time - no mean performance against this slim goalkeeper, who must rank among the best in the country."

City went on to face Middlesbrough in front of 40,179 fans in the third round although Bly was injured, but he was hitting the high spots again when they revisited Southport for a League game on Christmas Day, 1947. The Tigers' coach and kit went missing during an overnight stay in Liverpool and they had to play in black-and-white shirts, Southport's old colours, and charter a second vehicle for the game even though everything later turned up safely. But it did not deter them and it was recorded: "Billy Bly received an ovation on leaving the field as Hull City finished victors by two goals to one in a great struggle at Southport. The second half was a hotly-contested affair, in which Bly was the hero with many remarkable saves."

And even when City were beaten 4-1 at Chester in March 1948 - they had lost 5-1 in the corresponding game the previous season - he was at the hub of the action, as goalkeepers so often are in times of trouble. It was reported: "In the Hull goal Bly gave a capable display and his clean handling and good anticipation kept the score lower than it might have been." Another report noted: "Four goals were shot past Bly into the Hull City net at Chester last night, but, despite this, he was the star of the match. The Hull defence, with the exception of Bly, were inclined to falter under pressure. The goalkeeper, however, made a number of superb saves and it was just as well that he was in such excellent form because the home forwards were a constant menace."

Ten days later, on Easter Saturday, 1948, Bly was again inspired in a goalless draw away to Oldham Athletic. One report indicated: "Bly had a good day. He played magnificently and was instrumental in getting rid of many dangerous attacks." Another one stated: "Billy Bly, Hull City's young goalkeeper, had 15,000 fans gasping at Oldham. His was a breathtaking performance, including three back-breaking saves worthy of Frank Swift. He threw himself at the feet of forwards and his uncanny anticipation and faultless handling made Oldham fans agree with those who claim that Bly is an international prospect. This match would not have been a no-goal draw but for Bly's checking of three goal-deserving efforts from Billy Jessop."

The 1947-48 season, which finished with a 3-1 home win for City over Carlisle United when Bly saved a 33rd-minute penalty from Dick Burke, had produced plenty of optimism overall. But it was a season in which Billy Bly began to realise his immense potential with a series of significant performances. He made his 50th League appearance for the club on March 29, 1948, when he kept a clean sheet in a 3-0 win at home to New Brighton. It signalled the end of the three-match Easter programme and a seminal change in the club's fortunes. City appointed a player-coach to assist Buckley by the next match as they paid £6,000 for former England international inside-forward Raich Carter from Derby County. They were good times for Billy Bly and they were going to get even better now.

Carter's arrival was inspirational for the fans. There had been a crowd of 21,860 for the New Brighton game: Carter's debut in the next fixture - against York City - brought an attendance of 32,466, then the highest home League gate in the Tigers' history. Carter played in four of the final six games of the season, after which Buckley, who had been close to leaving City to join Leeds United the previous autumn, resigned. The relationship between him and the board had become tense, Leeds still wanted his services and this time he opted to join them. Coach George Lax initially took charge of team affairs after Buckley's departure had been announced with five League games remaining, but there was only one serious candidate to replace him on a long-term basis - Carter.

Billy Bly's career was now on the up and so were Hull City's fortunes as they prepared for a close-season trip to Scandinavia. It was to be the dawn of a glorious era for the Tigers as they took the Third Division North by storm in 1948-49. Carter immediately awarded 28-year-old Bly a pay rise as his basic wage touched the £10-per-week mark for the first time. The deal, from August 1, 1948, to July 31, 1949, also included a further £12 a week if he were in the first team as well as "bonuses as allowed by the League." And the signatures of Bly and Carter, both of whom were from the North-East and both of whom were to become two of the most popular players in the club's history, appeared, of course, on the same contract for the first time.

Carter immediately had a clear-out and abandoned the constant team changes of Buckley's time in charge so that City used just 22 players in 1948-49. In addition, it all revolved round 11 of them for most of the season with a largely injury-free Bly in goal and Jack Taylor, Tom Berry, Jimmy Greenhalgh, Harold Meens, Allan Mellor, Ken Harrison, Carter, Norman Moore, Viggo Jensen and Eddie Burbanks in front of him. Willie Buchan played in a little more than half the games, but the only other significant contributions came from Norman Fowler and Denis Durham. Jensen and Burbanks were Carter's only two new signings of the regulars.

The end-product was stunning. The Tigers won their first nine League games of the 1948-49 season to set a Football League record and went on a relentless march to the Third Division North title. They lost only one of their first 24 League matches, all of which featured Bly, and attracted an attendance of 49,655 to Boothferry Park on Christmas Day 1948 when they beat

Rotherham United, their only close rivals, 3-2. They went on to win 27 of their 42 League fixtures throughout the season and lost only four, putting together unbeaten runs of 11, 12 and seven matches twice. City conceded just 28 goals throughout the League season and Bly, who was made an honorary member of Wheeler Street Youth Club in Hull on December 6, 1948, played in 38 of the matches.

City scored 28 goals and conceded just six in the nine-match run at the start of the season, but it was not safe to assume that Bly had a comparatively easy life in goal and did not play his part in helping to set the record. His display in the sixth game of the sequence - a 3-0 victory at home to Wrexham - was praised by leading journalist Capel Kirby: "Hull will maintain their promotion drive only if they rid themselves of a fade-out complex. It came and there was many an occasion when Bly's acrobatics in the City goal saved them. Bly, already injured on one occasion, saved a certainty. He had run out, only partially saved and then at great risk made a backward dive to catch the ball as Wrexham's three inside-forwards converged for the kill."

And when the Tigers won 2-1 away to Accrington Stanley to make it nine wins out of nine from the start of the campaign and break a 45-year-old record, they did not have it all their own way. Tom Simms reported: "Accrington could not get the point they well deserved chiefly because of the alertness and clever anticipation of goalkeeper Bly and the stubbornness of Meens at centre-half." Another report commented: "Bly was brilliant in goal and Meens was a tower of strength."

City did enough to earn themselves a triumphant homecoming to Hull amid what were described as scenes of overwhelming enthusiasm involving about 12,000 fans. They stopped to dine in Ilkley on their way back, sang cherrily as the journey continued and were then greeted by police radio cars and motorcycle outriders on reaching Hull's boundary en route for the city's Regal Cinema in Ferensway. They were said to have received a tumultuous ovation when they appeared on the Regal's canopy as chairman Harold Needler and player-manager Carter made speeches to which civic heads responded. Finally trainer George Lax led the players in a rendition of Carter's theme song "When Your Hair has Turned to Silver." The Tigers had won nothing yet, but they were on their way, they had continued to attract record League attendances to Boothferry Park and Bly and Meens, the two longest-serving players, were enjoying some happy times with their colleagues.

The winning run ended with a goalless draw at Doncaster Rovers, but a week later the Tigers won 2-0 away to Hartlepools United and Bly enjoyed a nostalgic reunion before the game. Instead of staying overnight with his teammates in Saltburn, he met up with former City winger Jimmy Keen, who was also from Walker and had played for Walker Celtic. In fact, one of his relatives, wing-half Errington Keen, who was also born in Walker, had briefly been on City's books with Bly in the immediate postwar period towards the end of his career, during which he had played four times for England.

City suffered their first defeat of the season when a record home League crowd of 43,801 saw them lose 1-0 to Darlington and then came a 1-1 draw at Rochdale when it was recorded that "Bly had to be at his best in the face of their resolute attack." And then it was back to winning ways as Danish international Viggo Jensen scored in a 4-1 triumph at home to New Brighton. Jensen ensured immediate star status when he also scored in his next two matches, both of which were won, and, when a goalless draw at Gresty Road then followed, it was reported: "Exceptional goalkeeping by Bly largely accounted for Hull City collecting a point at Crewe. He was never better than in the closing stages. Once he ran well out to take the ball almost from Alf Clarke's toes. Then he was injured in stopping another blinder from the Crewe centre-forward."

There were two vital games against Rotherham during the Christmas period and the Tigers had to battle all the way to a goalless draw at Millmoor two days after beating them 3-2 at home. And reporter Geoff Beane noted: "'Keeper Bly was here, there and everywhere, parrying shots, keeping out Jack Shaw's headers with that safe pair of hands and generally contributing to Rotherham's frustration."

City gained extra momentum early in 1949 when Bill Price scored three goals in his first two games for the club, but in mid-February they lost their unbeaten away record when they went down 4-2 at Bradford City. But they then lost only one of their next 15 League games as promotion and then the Third Division North championship were in the bag. During that sequence Bly, who missed just four games because of injuries that season, conceded just one goal in one run of six games and then kept clean sheets for four matches on the trot.

Leading playwright Alan Plater, a long-established City devotee and originally from the North-East himself, summed up the mood of the time beautifully in an article for the Sunday Times many years later: "These days Raich Carter'd be called a left-sided midfield player, but in truth he reinvented the game as he went along. He didn't play the game: he presided over it. He took all the corners and throw-ins on either side of the field and also turned up on the goal-line when necessary, helping Billy Bly to defend a one-goal lead and the latest fracture."

And right-winger Ken Harrison, City's only ever-present player during the 1948-49 season, reflected: "Raich Carter would take throw-ins and he threw the ball above me. This was so that the opposing defence could clear for us to pick the ball up deep in our half and then build up a move into the opponents' half. Sometimes Carter would throw the ball to me when opponents expected it to be thrown high! I would then return the ball to him so that he could play it into space. Carter told you what and how he wanted you to play and had players passing and running and playing into space. My main strength was speed and, although I would have preferred playing at inside-forward, we grew as a team and gained experience."

Even though the Tigers were attracting huge crowds at the time, Harrison also talked of the players' almost-disarming approach towards going to Boothferry Park on match days: "I used to live next door to Billy in a club house down Worcester Road and he, Harold Meens and I used to have a leisurely stroll down to the ground. Harold lived around the corner and Denis Durham and Allan Mellor lived in Danube Road. They were all club houses and we all walked together to the ground."

Bly's wife, Dorothy, added: "A lot of the players lived there. There was Harold Meens, Henry Brown, who came from Wolves with Maj. Buckley, Ernie Bell and Dai Davies. One of the goalies, Alec Corbett, a big, ginger-haired Scotsman, lived next door, as did Kenny Harrison, who used to play with Raich. It was great because Roy grew up with many of their sons.

"On match days the players and their wives used to walk down to the ground. The streets were thick with people going to the games. There were just crowds and crowds of people and the atmosphere was wonderful."

Bly, in fact, had a lucky charm during the 1948-49 promotion season - curious for someone whose career had been repeatedly cursed by bad luck with injuries - because he insisted on wearing a tattered blue-and-white shirt, which was a relic from his schooldays, under his jersey. He believed that it helped him when playing in goal! "I wouldn't be happy without it. I've had the shirt since since I played for West Walker School in Newcastle and, as a mascot, I believe it's helped me a lot," he insisted. Similarly, Billy had a further superstition because he always knew his place in the team when it came to running out into the stadia for matches. "I always like to be 10th on the pitch," he said.

At any rate it all worked a treat because City not only shone in the League in 1948-49, but they also had a memorable run in the FA Cup. It started quietly with a 3-1 win at home to Accrington Stanley and a 2-1 victory in a replay at Reading, who were among the front-line challengers for promotion from the Third Division South. But then it gained impetus with three pieces of giant-killing in successive rounds.

In the third round the Tigers were drawn away at Second Division Blackburn Rovers and Bly received a welcome telegram on the day of the match. It was sent to him care of Blackburn Rovers, it simply said: "All the best, Bill" and significantly it came from his old colleague and mentor, George Maddison. City won 2-1 after extra time and the headlines included: "Bly and Greenhalgh stars of cuptie." Greenhalgh was making the most of a return to his native Lancashire, while it was said of Bly: "It must be conceded that Blackburn had the greater shooting opportunities, but between them and success lay Billy Bly, who saved at all angles when they were not at fault themselves with their markmanship. There were times when the ball ran none too well for Blackburn and yet it was Bly's brilliance, coupled with strong supporting defensive work by colleagues, that contributed more to their undoing than did anything else." In addition, Tom Markland wrote under the headline "Bly was Hull City hero" that he should "hand out full marks to Billy Bly for a most accomplished and courageous display. It was he who held the bridge when Rovers were at their best towards the close of the second half, leaping to one shot here and diving to another shot there." Another account stated: "Bly must take the bouquets for a super show before and after Blackburn's goal. The readiness of their danger man, Dennis Westcott, to shoot called for Bly's best and there were cheers all the way for Hull's goalkeeper. As the game progressed, City gathered strength from his inspiring lead." And Arthur Shrive wrote: "The Hull defence did not always cover up astutely and left openings for the opposition, which were frustrated by the clever goalkeeping of Bly. He made two of the best saves of the match from high-power free-kicks taken by Bob Pryde from outside the penalty area."

Norman Moore scored City's extra-time winner and he was twice on target against his home-town club in the fourth round when they beat Second Division Grimsby Town 3-2 at Blundell Park. Carter, who had been doubtful for the game, scored City's other goal, but it was also reported: "City were the cooler team and, to a man, they stuck to their guns magnificently with Bly a never-failing rearguard."

First Division Stoke City, then led by Neil Franklin, an England international who was later to join the Tigers, lay in store next at the Victoria Ground and it was stated in one preview of the fifth-round tie: "Goalkeeper Billy Bly is on the small side, but probably among the best half-dozen in the game today." There was heavy rain shortly before the start and City picked up some injuries during the game - notably to Viggo Jensen and goalscorers Moore and Greenhalgh - but Bly again had his moments: "Stoke never had a shot at goal in the first half, but were more aggressive later. It was then that City showed the same sureness in defence as attack, Bly pulling off a spectacular save from one of George Mountford's specials." A further report said: "Freddie Steele bore down on the Hull goal with only Bly ahead, but the goalkeeper ran to the edge of the penalty area to make a spectacular save by diving and covering. Bly came in for another great ovation five minutes later when Steele looked like having another big chance. This time Bly dived across his goal to punch vigorously with his right fist as Steele made his smashing shot." It was also recorded: "Bly, in the Hull goal, had comparatively little to do for most of the game, but he did make two spectacular saves at a period when Stoke looked more likely to get on top than at any other time."

On the morning of the game, in fact, Billy had discovered that he had extra competition for the goalkeeping berth. His deputy, Alec Corbett, was on the transfer list at his own request, so the Tigers announced the signing of Blackpool's unsettled goalkeeper Joe Robinson, who had played in the previous season's FA Cup final, which Manchester United had won 4-2. In keeping with the established club tradition, he came from the North-East, too, because he was originally from Pegswood in Northumberland. Carter, meanwhile, was said to have shrugged off the signing as "making sure of suitable duplication for when the hard matches come along."

And there was a bit of a bonus for Billy in the aftermath of the triumph at Stoke. He got home from the match to receive a congratulatory telegram from his family in Newcastle. It read: "Well done! Hope to see you at Wembley! All our best wishes - Mum, Dad, Hilda and Tom."

Curiously the draw for the 1948-49 quarter-finals then threw up a home tie for the Tigers against holders United as their season's momentum continued to build impressively and dramatically. The tie was to provide one of the greatest occasions in the club's history as a record gate of 55,019 filled Boothferry Park and Dorothy Bly recalled the splendour of it all: "It was just thick with people and they were packed in like sardines." Billy himself received several goodwill messages, which again underlined the importance of the telegram in those days when faxes, e-mails and mobile telephones could not even have been anticipated. One telegram to Billy was sent by Bill Fenwick, from Ramsbotton, and read: "Good luck to you all this afternoon! Up the Tigers!" An Aldershot couple sent a simple message of: "Best of luck!" and someone describing himself as a Walkerite from Whitstable said: "Good old Walker! All the best, Billy!" And a message of: "Best of luck in Cup!" was sent from a well-wisher from Glasgow. The fact that the telegrams were sent to Billy personally showed the particular esteem in which supporters held him and the extent of the hero worship that he had been accorded.

As it was, United won the tie 1-0 and there was controversy about their 73rd-minute winner when two internationals, Scotland's Jimmy Delaney and England's Stan Pearson, the goalscorer, combined because there were claims that the ball had gone dead in the build-up. The other big drama surrounded Bly because he carried on playing with a broken nose: "Henry Cockburn's free-kick caused a fierce goalmouth melee, in which the advancing Bly missed the ball as he dived amid a forest of attackers. He was injured and lay prostrate for a while. Bly had obvious-ly been shaken badly and, although he resumed, he was nursing his head for some time." Another account recorded: "If there are any medals for sixth-round·FA Cup players, then Hull City's Billy Bly must qualify. For 54 agonising minutes he played on after he had broken his nose. Halftime first aid enabled him to come out for the second half, but he appeared to be so dazed that full-back Jack Taylor guided him to the goal. How he managed to play on and make saves is a secret known only to the great heart of this slightly-built, fearless goalkeeper." Bly suffered concussion and one report asserted that he "played almost automatically." City emerged as gallant heroes despite their defeat and it was noted: "Bly needed all his agility against lightning thrusts."

Such was Bly's popularity that he began to be in demand for personal appearances to make presentations in 1949. One was at Buckingham Street Boys' School in East Hull when they were the joint holders of the Ferens Charity Cup. On another occasion he again ventured into East Hull to hand over football trophies at Southcoates Lane Junior School. Ironically, the winner of the Brunswick Memorial Cup was Jimmy Duncan, who later became one of his teammates at Boothferry Park when City won promotion from the new Third Division 10 years later.

There was also an occasion on which Carter and Bly were hauled out of their after-match bath "to acknowledge the cheers of a wildly-excited crowd wanting to show their appreciation of men who had played a big part in leading the club back into the Second Division." Billy, for his part, relished playing behind his teammates during that memorable season and he later admitted: "They were the best League team I played in. I had so little to do and so much time to do it in."

At the end of the season Hull's Lord Mayor, Ald. Thomas Broadbent, held a civic dinner at the city's Guildhall "to celebrate the promotion of Hull City Association Football Club to the Second Division." It took place on Monday, May 9, and Billy and Dorothy duly attended as Carter responded to the Lord Mayor's toast to the club's manager and players. In fact, Billy and Dorothy signed their menu, as did Norman Moore, Norman Fowler and Stan Kirk and their respective wives, Joyce, Madge and Edna.

In 1949-50 City carried on where they had left off for a while and there was even a hint of a second successive promotion. They began with a 3-2 home win over Bury on the opening day and Bly soon found his form. It was reported: "A top-speed Bury attack would have made a big mark on the scoresheet if goalkeeper Billy Bly had not barred their way. Billy was so brilliant that Hull fans say that he's just the man to catch the eye of the England selectors as Frank Swift drops out." The Tigers won 16 out of their first 27 games in the Second Division up to the end of January 1950 and the gates at Boothferry Park regularly topped the 40,000 mark. An attendance of 47,638 saw Bly keep a clean sheet as the Tigers beat Leeds United 1-0 with a goal by Jensen and there were 48,447 at Boothferry Park when he did it again in a 2-0 victory over Brentford during the Christmas period.

Teammate Denis Durham, whose appearances had been restricted by polio, still recalled the tremendous following that the City had at that time and the atmosphere created by the interest in the team: "There was no television and the War hadn't been over all that long, so many people were attracted to football in those days - more so than now. It was quite a feeling to go out in front of those big attendances, but it became the every-day norm. It was natural and it was unheard-of to have the kind of small attendances you get nowadays."

But the 1949-50 season was quirky at times because Bly let in six goals in a first-team game for the first time even though City won 12 of their first 18 games. It came in a 6-2 defeat at Sheffield Wednesday in front of 52,403 fans, but a fortnight later he was the hero as the Tigers got back on to the winning trail. They won 4-1 away to Queen's Park Rangers and it was reported: "Carter was the man of the match. He was really magnificent and, if anyone ran him close for honours, it was Bly. He pulled off some great saves before City really got going and helped in the demoralisation of Rangers."

A fortnight later Eddie Burbanks got the winner in a 2-1 success at the then Swansea Town in curious circumstances because Billy set off for the long trip to the game without his cap and his wife, Dorothy, had to send it along with the fans later on! It was still noted: "Burbanks and Bly were the outstanding men on the field. Swansea still had hopes of maintaining their home record to the bitter end. When they did take their chances, however, Bly was there to thwart them."

Bly saved a penalty by George Stobbart with "a wonderful cat-like spring across goal" in a 3-0 victory away to Luton Town and he again stood out in a 3-1 victory against Plymouth Argyle at Home Park in January 1950. It was recorded: "Plymouth might have been in an unassailable position by the interval but for one player, Hull City's goalkeeper Bly. At least two of the speculative Plymouth shots that did find the mark would have beaten many other goalkeepers, but the acrobatic Bly saved brilliantly."

But the wheels came off the wagon after City's undignified FA Cup exit at home to Third Division North side Stockport County in the fourth round even though there was a crowd of 50,103 for the 1-1 draw with Sheffield Wednesday at Boothferry Park two days later. Bly did a lot to earn the Tigers a third-round replay against Southport, which they won 5-0. But it was reported of the first meeting, which ended 0-0: "Hull were lucky to draw and owe their chance of a replay to a wonderful display by goalkeeper Bly, who saved his side time and again after the defence had blundered. Southport had several scoring chances, but Bly's superb form robbed them of a victory they deserved."

And even though the Tigers lost their replay at home to Stockport 2-0, they would probably not have even got that far without Bly's intervention in the first meeting - another goalless draw. James Holland wrote: "Only two players, Hull City goalkeeper Billy Bly and Stockport County's inside-right Alec Herd, can look back upon the game with any personal satisfaction. Bly, who must be one of the best uncapped 'keepers playing today, undoubtedly stood between Stockport and the victory which they should have gained. A brilliant save from a Herd header in the first half was the most notable of many fine efforts." Tom Markland added: "I must hand it to Bly for the masterly save he made from Herd's header, which seemed to have 'goal' written all over it. Bly timed his dive perfectly and his goalkeeping throughout bore the hallmark of confidence and fearlessness. I have yet to see him play a bad game." Even the peerless Kenneth Wolstenholme got in on the act: "In the face of heavy pressure the Hull defence produced a star who shone more brightly even than Alec Herd - goalkeeper Billy Bly. He gave one of the best goalkeeping displays I have seen for a long time. He made two sensational saves from Tom Swinscoe."

Amid the cupties, journalist John Macadam singled out Bly for special praise in his column in the Daily Express: "He is a goalkeeper with the agility of a monkey, the strength of a tiger despite his slight frame and a sense of anticipation that we do not recall noting since we cast fond eyes upon Harry Hibbs. There has been a lot of talk of goalkeeping possibles, but in this humble opinion Billy Bly, of Hull City, is an England international certainty. He cannot be ignored from either the safety or the spectacular point of view."

Bly maintained his standards and missed only four games because of injury after a 1-0 defeat against Grimsby Town at Blundell Park. Even then he did well because it was recorded: "Hull City goalkeeper Billy Bly was in top form at Grimsby. Three times he was knocked out in making desperate saves and now inside-forward Don Revie must be wondering why he did not accept easy chances that might have turned Bly's performance into a victory."

Near the end of the season Bly again showed his battling spirit when he saved a penalty in a 2-0 defeat away to Coventry City, blocked the rebound and was beaten only at the third attempt. It was still reported: "Had it not been for a grand display in goal by Billy Bly, the score would have been far greater. Time and time again Bly stood between Coventry and further goals, leaving his charge to take shots from all directions. On one occasion he took a drive from Peter Murphy full in the face."

The Tigers won only one of their last 15 League games and finished a respectable seventh in the table, but there was a fascinating little vignette during the Easter period just before the visit to Coventry. Tottenham Hotspur had been out of the top flight since 1934-35, but they were on their way back in 1949-50 and were winging their way to the Second Division championship - which they eventually won by nine points - when they met City twice during Easter. On April 7, 1950 - Good Friday morning - the Tigers went to White Hart Lane and drew 0-0 against a Spurs side containing Ted Ditchburn, Alf Ramsey, Bill Nicholson, Les Medley, Harry Clarke and Eddie Baily, all of whom played for England as full internationals, and Welsh international wing-half Ron Burgess. Bly distinguished himself and Gerry Bowler bottled up dangerous Channel Islander Len Duquemin so that City drew 0-0. In addition, it all took place in front of a crowd of 66,889 - the biggest gate ever for any game involving Hull City. In fact, FA supremo Sir Stanley Rous, snooker player Joe Davis and commentator Raymond Glendenning were among the throng.

Bly was in his element and was the Tigers' saviour because it was noted: "A moment or two before the end Les Bennett brushed by Gerry Bowler and found only Billy Bly ahead. It was a dramatic moment of great peril - a moment when it seemed as if Spurs were going to snatch a last-minute victory - but instantaneous action by City's goalkeeper made the game safe. He came out at speed just wide of his goal to meet the lone attacker and made one of his characteristic, daring dives at Bennett's feet." Renowned soccer journalist Desmond Hackett wrote: "Hull goalkeeper Billy Bly was a cross between a Hampstead Heath contortionist and an Olympic Games diver in saving efforts from Medley." And writer W. J. Hicks added: "Gerry Bowler and the lithe, jack-in-the-box goalkeeper Billy Bly gave the match its only exciting qualities. They shone as brightly as the morning sunshine and Bly handled the ball with the confidence of an international."

City drew 2-2 at home to West Ham United the following day and then came the return clash against Spurs at Boothferry Park on Easter Monday. This time the Tigers won 1-0 and Scottish forward Fred Smith scored what turned out to be his only senior goal for the club. It meant, though, that Bly had twice kept a clean sheet against that rampant Tottenham side in a matter of days. Spurs, after all, scored a total of 81 goals in their 40 other League games that season, so it was not often that they were kept at bay.

It also meant that there was still plenty to cheer for City fans even if it were not a promotion season. Bly played in 38 of the 42 League games and, although there were some heavy defeats and it was ultimately a season of anti-climax, there were many other high spots to savour, such as keeping a clean sheet in a 1-0 home win over Leeds United and doing the double over Leicester City. Curiously, though, Bly had not received a pay rise for promotion: he was still on a basic £10 a week with a further £12 for being in the first team. But in two seasons he had built a formidable reputation for himself and it was a testimony to his astonishing progress that he was repeatedly being touted for international recognition.

The Tigers were never to capitalise fully on the impact and progress that they made from 1948 to 1950 and Bly himself missed most of the 1950-51 season because of injury. In fact, he was involved in nearly as many club dinners as first-team matches. There was City Supporters' Club's pre-season dinner at the Goodfellowship Inn in Hull on August 10, 1950, and the following month there was a welcoming dinner at Hull Guildhall for top Turkish club

Galatasaray, who were beaten 2-0 at Boothferry Park on September 11 by goals from Alf Ackerman and Gordon Inwood. On March 13, 1951, City's vice-presidents held a dinner on behalf of the club at Jackson's Restaurant in Hull when toasts were proposed by FA secretary Sir Stanley Rous and international referee Arthur Ellis. Bly, meanwhile, played only five first-team games that season, but he was soon back to the fore. He continued to gain personal respect even though the club began a run of five seasons of struggle that ended in relegation in 1955-56.

Bly's own reputation, though, remained high from the outset of the 1951-52 season when City drew 0-0 at Barnsley. It was noted: "Billy Bly, so often hailed as a front-rank man, lost his League place last October with one of his numerous fractures, but his comeback against Barnsley must have gladdened the heart of manager Raich Carter. Bly alone prevented ace marksman Cecil McCormack from collecting a hat-trick."

Bly began to have another good season and he soon attracted attention from different parts of the soccer world. The following month City lost 4-0 against Notts County at Meadow Lane and the famed Bill Shankly was among the crowd. Then the manager of Grimsby Town, he admitted to admiring Bly and commented afterwards: "He is a great goalkeeper - certainly one of the best."

Bly also turned in another peerless performance in October 1951 in a 2-0 defeat by Leeds United at Elland Road. One report commented: "Leeds United would have scored almost at will if it hadn't been for Billy Bly. One save was made while Billy was on his knees: but really the rest of the Hull team should have gone on their knees for the services the goalkeeper rendered." Another report indicated: "Billy Bly has been guarding the Hull City goal for 14 years and he looked good enough at Leeds to keep his place for a long time yet. City had much to thank the capable Geordie for as he saved shots from all angles."

The Tigers were on a run of 12 League games without a win and the following month Bly gained more plaudits in a 1-0 defeat against Leicester City at Filbert Street. It was recorded: "Cast-iron goalkeeper Billy Bly saved Hull from their heaviest defeat with the best goalkeeping display seen on the ground this season. It wasn't bad shooting that kept the scoring down to Arthur Rowley's decider - just inspired goalkeeping from Bly, who finished tired and bruised, but still resolute." Another account insisted: "Hull City are indeed in the doldrums and were moderate in every position but one because Bly, their goalkeeper, has never played a better game. He was at home to all kinds of shots and in the first half they were going at him from all angles. Some of the low shots he saved were worthy of the best international form. Leicester perhaps should have improved their goal average, but Bly was so good that there were really only two occasions on which the forwards could be accused of missing gilt-edged chances." And reporter Billy King wrote: "Leicester City were the bosses from the start, but they found Billy Bly, the visiting goalkeeper, in his most daring mood. Time and time again he thwarted the Leicester forwards and earned the cheers of the crowd for his skilful saves and courageous interceptions. It was a great display of goalkeeping at its best. At the end players clapped him on the back and the crowd rose to him as he left the field." It was also reported: "If Hull had got away with a point, all bonus money should have gone to goalkeeper Billy Bly. He kept them in the game right to the last minute and his wonderful anticipation upset innumerable home moves." And another report indicated: "Daring Billy Bly put on a goalkeeping act for Hull City that has not been bettered at Leicester this season. He alone stopped Leicester from getting more than the only goal of the game and players joined spectators in a roaring, clapping ovation as Bly left the field."

Billy just kept going as the Tigers failed to capitalise on the optimism of the Carter era although injuries held him back a lot between 1952 and 1954. But there were personal high spots for Bly as he worked with Bob Jackson, Carter's successor. Being a goalkeeper meant out of necessity that there were times when Bly the individual was a hero on occasions when City the team lost. One such occasion was in the FA Cup in 1953-54. City beat Brentford at the third attempt in the third round and then took on Blackburn Rovers in three successive games. Bly was injured in the first game in the League when they lost 3-1 against a Rovers side who were among the Second Division contenders. Tommy Forgan replaced him for the first cuptie, which ended in a 2-2 draw at Ewood Park, but Bly was back for the replay at Boothferry Park when the Tigers won 2-1 with goals by Brian Bulless and Alf Ackerman. And it was reported: "The return of Bly tended to encourage defensive confidence and it was to his credit that, although his nose was broken only 12 days previously, he went as wholeheartedly and effectively into the fray as ever."

The Tigers were then drawn at home to Tottenham Hotspur in the fifth round and 46,839 packed Boothferry Park for an incident-packed game. City had to play with 10 men after Ken Harrison was injured in a challenge with Spurs' George Robb in only the third minute and was found to have fractured his kneecap after he had been carried off on a stretcher. Spurs tried to take advantage and Bly was at his best to deny "Sonny" Walters and Les Bennett. In fact, it was noted: "So impressed was Bennett with Bly's recovery and clearance that he shook hands with the Tigers' goalkeeper." In the end Eddie Baily put Tottenham ahead, but Viggo Jensen made it 1-1 when he equalised with a last-minute penalty after he himself had been fouled to earn City their fourth draw of the season in the FA Cup.

The draw for the quarter-finals had taken place and the winners of the replay were to visit West Bromwich Albion. It would have been a plum draw for the Tigers because that season Albion were a powerful side because they were to win the FA Cup and also finish as the runners-up to their close rivals Wolverhampton Wanderers in the First Division.

The replay duly took place on February 24, 1954, and attracted 52,936 to White Hart Lane. Spurs won 2-0 thanks to a 23rd-minute header from Walters and a last-minute goal from Baily after a backpass by Neil Franklin, making his first cup appearance of the season, had gone astray. But only one player was acknowledged as the man-of-the-match because Billy Bly had one of his finest hours and a half despite finishing on the losing side.

It was reported: "Any glory which Tottenham may derive from their 2-0 cuptie defeat of Hull City must be equalled or even transcended by the goalkeeping display given by Billy Bly. There can be no doubt that Spurs deserved to win, but standing between them and a more decisive margin was the defiant Bly, whose performance was really epic. He was tested from all angles and heights by an opposition far more resolute and effective than they had been at Boothferry Park on Saturday, but the acrobatic and daring Billy defied all-comers with his wonderful anticipation and positioning. Bly's saves were too numerous for an individual record of them, but he frustrated Spurs so often that there was second-half evidence of their despairing. It was obvious that the way in which Bly was foiling them was having a shaking effect on their morale besides inspiring City, who had had a disappointing first half, to better things."

Journalist Jack Wood wrote: "Billy Bly, that homely, much-battered character of Yorkshire soccer, won the cheers and the hearts of a near-53,000 Tottenham crowd with a superb goalkeeping display. Bly the Brave, whose personal injury list reads like a one-man casualty communique, saved Hull from a humiliating Cup farewell and the afternoon for everyone present. Without him there would be little to remember. Onlookers cheered his every kick as the game went on and the list of his goalkeeping deeds grew. They stayed at the end to cheer him from the field. Luck was with him at times, but without him the score might easily have risen to eight."

And national newspaperman John Macadam was equally as fulgent in his praise: "As long as they talk football Tottenham way, they'll talk not so much about how Spurs knocked Hull out of the FA Cup as of how goalkeeper Billy Bly defied them. It was an inspired piece of goalkeeping that deserved a better fate. Bly saved long shots and short, point-blank shots, high ones and screamers along the ground and the twice he was beaten had nothing to do with him - nothing whatever. The crowd knew well that they were in the presence of greatness. As the knowledge grew, they cheered his every step. At the end they rose to him as one man and gave him a personal ovation all the way off the field. Well they might. Billy Bly is one of the unluckiest goalkeepers in the business. He has broken almost every bone available, even to 'rubber' men such as himself, yet there he was with superb confidence, tipping the ball over the bar and round the post, diving at onrushing feet and positioning himself like a master. But for him Spurs might have won by at least 4-0 and I wish to see nothing better than his performance. What will be told for a long time is the tale of the greatness of Bly."

Brian Bulless, a good friend and a teammate in the two cupties, summed it up when he added: "I was 19 and in the RAF when I was first chosen for the first team. But not long afterwards I was in the team who drew the great Tottenham Hotspur at home in the FA Cup. After a 1-1 draw at Boothferry Park, we went to London for the replay and Billy Bly played the game of his life even though we lost 2-0. We played together many times after that, but it will always be remembered as one of Bill's greatest performances."

And Andy Davidson said: "I was injured, but I watched the game from the stand. The funniest thing concerned Spurs' second goal. Neil Franklin was a great player, but he used to try the most outrageous things on the ball inside his own penalty box. This time he back-heeled the ball towards where he thought Billy was, but it caught him out. Billy went berserk about the goal, which wasn't surprising because he'd just played the game of his life!"

It was the same story in the FA Cup the following season when the Tigers lost 2-0 at home to Birmingham City in the third round on January 8, 1955. Bly was brought back for the tie after a rare occasion on which he had been dropped from the first team. He soon made his impact because it was noted: "Hull's hero was veteran 'keeper Billy Bly, recalled from the reserves. Neither goal could be held against him and he saved magnificently under tremendous Birmingham pressure."

City did not play for another month, but Bly was back with a vengeance and had a point to prove. This time it was in a 2-1 League win at Middlesbrough and it was recorded: "Allow for some wonder saves by Billy Bly, the cool generalship of Neil Franklin and a few master moves by Wilf Mannion and it was Middlesbrough who dug their own graves in losing their first League game at home since mid-September. They made an all-out effort to save the game in the last five minutes and that was when Bly did his stuff, which enabled Hull to walk off with the points. Bly earned the man-of-the-match tag when he thwarted Middlesbrough's late rally, which might have brought them two quick goals against a less capable 'keeper."

The game brought a spot of controversy when Middlesbrough claimed that Bly was over the line with the ball three minutes from time when he leaned back to collect a shot from Arthur Fitzsimons and he was involved another quirky situation a fortnight later because City lost 2-0 away to Rotherham United and he was beaten by two own goals - from Viggo Jensen and Tom Berry! Journalist John Fulton, though, praised Bly's contribution: "His daring and meticulous timing had Rotherham United players scratching their heads and wondering just what they would have to do to get the ball past him. Bly threw himself at every ball despite the hard ground and held it in the same way as a youngster grabs his most precious toy from covetous eyes."

And as Bly's experience and reputation grew during the 1950s, it seemed that he had some favourites grounds where he repeatedly turned out to be at his most defiant. Plymouth Argyle's Home Park was one example. He was on top form in City's 2-1 win at Home Park in October 1954 and it was reported: "Four games at Plymouth since the War have brought Hull seven points. Every time Bly has upset Plymouth's victory plans." Another account added: "The Plymouth crowd will want to forget the name of Billy Bly. Two seasons ago he came to Plymouth and robbed Argyle of victory with a brilliant display of goalkeeping. This time he repeated the performance and Hull retained their unbeaten home record. When Plymouth's forwards pressed repeatedly before halftime, Bly spoiled their afternoon with another top-of-the-table performance. He cut out crosses with skill and made six international-class saves." A further report indicated: "Man of the match was Hull goalkeeper Bly, who has always played well in Plymouth. He has never played a bad game at Home Park and was in his usual Plymouth form." Even the Pilgrims' manager Jimmy Rae admitted: "Those near-miracle saves from Bly must have been enough to break the heart of our centre-forward Neil Langman. We would have had four or five goals but for Bly's great work."

City finished 19th in the Second Division in 1954-55 and flirted with relegation until they won 1-0 at Fulham in mid-April when Bly again was the saviour. It was reported: "Billy Bly produced a magnificent display. He made the first of many great saves when he just beat Bedford Jezzard to the ball and then produced a masterly effort when Jezzard beat Tom Berry out on the left and centred to Bobby Robson, who then had only Bly to beat. Robson essayed a shot to the right-hand corner of the net, but Bly flung himself across goal to palm the ball round the post. Robson again brought the best out of Bly when he collected a shot that looked a winner all over. But the game never reached great heights except for Bly's display."

Bly had picked up the accolades on a regular basis throughout his career, but remained cool, calm and collected, always reflecting that he was just doing his job. He got his first taste of relegation in 1955-56 as the Carter era became a distant memory, but he coped with two more seasons in the Third Division North, helping the Tigers to qualify comfortably for the new Third Division when they finished fifth in 1957-58.

It meant that happy days were here again because he was given the opportunity to play in a second promotion campaign for the Tigers. On this occasion 38-year-old Bly made more League appearances in a season than at any other time during his City career, playing in 45 out of 46 games. The Tigers relied heavily on the goals of Bill Bradbury, whose 30 in the League remains a postwar club record, and Colin Smith, who also pointed out: "I played in the promotion team of 1958-59 with Bill and found him very dedicated to his fitness. He was a hell of a good goalkeeper, he was quiet and unassuming, his feet were firmly on the ground and he showed a willingness to help."

The season did not start well for City, who won only one of their first seven matches, culminating in a 6-1 defeat at Southampton when it was reported: "The Tigers defence - Bly apart - were hopelessly outclassed and cut to ribbons." But defender Paul Feasey then took over as captain and City never looked back after that. They won four games in succession and twice later in the season they won six matches on the trot. Their record at Boothferry Park was exemplary because they won 19 out of 23 of them, including 12 in succession at one stage. In the end they finished as runners-up behind Plymouth Argyle and clinched promotion in the penultimate game - at home to Bury, whom they beat 2-0. The game was played in torrential rain and there was a memorable photograph afterwards of a mud-spattered quartet of Bly, Brian Garvey, Paul Feasey and Frank Harrison enjoying a victory toast of champagne.

The new Third Division was a high-scoring affair in general, but the Tigers were the top goalscorers with 90. Their defensive record, though, was also good because they conceded 55 goals - the second-best in the division behind third-placed Brentford. It would have been even more impressive if it had not been for the six that they gave away at Southampton and a 5-1 defeat at Wrexham in the final match. Feasey later recalled: "The standard of football in the Third Division was a lot higher than ever before, so Hull City's feat in winning promotion was all the more noteworthy."

The Third Division championship had been at stake at Wrexham and there were stories that City's players and directors had had a dispute between clinching promotion against Bury and going to the Racecourse Ground. And the Tigers might have lost even more heavily then 5-1 because it was reported: "Wrexham might have doubled their score but for Bly's agility and daring. Three times Bly made back-breaking saves and twice he scooped the ball from forwards' toes when closer marking and firmer tackling would have saved all anxiety."

But full-back Denis Durham reflected: "It was one of those games. I seem to think that four of Wrexham's goals went in off the post. Luck was against us, but we'd still got enough points to cope and be promoted, so we were happy enough. It was a great feeling."

Winger Mike Bowering echoed the sentiment when he recalled the aftermath: "Wrexham were holding their club presentation evening after the match and we all went to it. We were staying over and my last recollection of Billy that night was of him walking down the street in a good mood with a bottle of whisky in his hand. And, from what I can remember, there were only about three players ready to get on the bus at the appointed time the following morning." Roy Bly simply confirms that Billy hardly ever drunk beer, but did like the odd tot of whisky, particularly on special occasions...

The Tigers finished one point behind Plymouth and four points clear of Brentford and Norwich City, who reached the FA Cup semi-finals and attracted the biggest gate of the season - 24,156 - to Boothferry Park that season on Easter Saturday, in third and fourth places respectively. The team were nicknamed Brocklebank's Toddlers after Manchester United's Busby Babes and Billy spoke of the club's revival under "the kindly and shrewd guidance" of manager Bob Brocklebank.

City would also have won the title if a controversial penalty - the players insisted that any infringement took place outside the area - had not been awarded against them in a 1-1 draw at Plymouth midway through the season. But such matters merely bonded the team closer together and most members of that promotion squad automatically talk of the youth, exuberance and camaraderie in their ranks.

In one sense Billy Bly might have been the exception because of his age, but right-winger Doug Clarke recalled: "Bill played a big role in the achievements of the 1958-59 season. The most lasting memories of that campaign are that the team we had were made up of a few lads, such as Mick Bowering, Paul Feasey and Colin Smith, who had just been brought in from local football. I have always maintained that the success we had was because of a good team spirit. If we had to stay overnight for away games, every one of us made sure that we stuck together and enjoyed each other's company, of which Bill was a big part."

And Bowering added: "In one of the games we lost - 2-1 at Chesterfield - there was a tackle on me, which Bob Brocklebank later said amounted to grievous bodily harm. All the lads ran across to help out and got involved. In fact, Andy Davidson ran over from about 50 yards away. The only one who didn't get caught up in it was Billy Bly because he was too far away and he was too much of a gentleman anyway! But that was how it was in that team - it was all for one and one for all. Where one went, everybody went. The team spirit was unbelievable."

Bly's long career with Hull City ended on a sour note when they were relegated back to the Third Division in 1959-60. But there was still evidence that he did not let his own standards slip at the age of 39. City won only two of their first 15 League games, but he was still at his best, for example, during a 1-0 defeat against Rotherham United at Millmoor. The Millers took the points with a 79th-minute goal by Brian Sawyer, but journalist Willie Lyon wrote: "United continually got through only to find evergreen Billy Bly an insurmountable obstacle in the Hull goal. Bly would not have been disgraced if another two or three goals had ben scored against him. But all the Bly heroics came to nothing in the end."

There might have been an overall feeling of anti-climax because of the way that Billy's career with Hull City ended, but it should never cloud the good times. There were two promotion seasons and there were numerous occasions when Billy Bly was a brave, heroic goalkeeper. He was merely plying his trade, but they gave him an inner satisfaction of a job well done and memories of lots of happy days.

8

The Down Side

Hull City have always been known as a yo-yo club and have ultimately had more downs than ups, so it would be natural that anybody who played for them for a considerable length of time would go through a fair few disappointments and emotions along the way. Billy Bly was no exception because promotion seasons with the club were duly counterbalanced by relegation campaigns, he was in giant-killing and giant-killed City teams in cupties, he repeatedly suffered serious injuries and he endured the ignominy of being dropped from the side.

Bly also made the occasional mistake, but he was consistently reliable by general goalkeeping standards and the law of averages dictates that things will not always go according to plan during a 23-year period. It was a 2-2 draw on promotion and relegation issues while Bly was with the Tigers and there were just two embarrassing occasions on which he played in FA Cup defeats in which they were humbled by lower-grade opposition. In both instances City were in the Second Division and were knocked out by Third Division North opposition. In the fourth round in 1949-50 City drew 0-0 away to Stockport County and then lost the replay 2-0 at Boothferry Park. And in 1952-53 Bly was also in the City team beaten 2-1 at home by Gateshead in the fourth round again.

But it would be unrealistic to expect that there would not be occasional setbacks at various stages and the most recurrent of them in his long career were surely the numerous injuries that would have demoralised a lesser person, but he bore the brunt of them stoically and viewed them philosophically as part of his job description. On a personal level, though, they still represented many of the more depressing times of his career because of their severity and regularity.

Bly's absences from the first team during his time with the Tigers were largely the legacy of those injuries, but there were darker moments when he was actually dropped from the side. After his initial foray into League football as a teenager in the latter stages of the 1938-39 season, he did not start the following season. Jack Curnow was in goal for the opening two League games of the season that ultimately never was when war broke out. But those matches in the Third Division never counted among official records because of the overriding world crisis.

But there were three postwar occasions when Bly was dropped from the side. That in itself represents only a small return for such a long stay at one club and speaks volumes for his consistency, but such occasions are always a particular blow to the pride of a player when he is regarded as an established first-teamer rather than someone who is perennially on the fringes and might accept the rough with the smooth a little more readily and phlegmatically.

By the time that Bly was dropped from City's side for the first time as an established senior player, he was 30 and had made more than 150 League appearances for the club. City had consolidated comfortably in 1949-50 on their return to the Second Division after promotion and finished seventh in the table. But their progress was not maintained in 1950-51, which was one of the most depressing seasons ever for Bly at Boothferry Park.

He played in the opening four League games, which yielded four points out of a possible eight, but City conceded a total of 11 goals in them. In the fourth game they lost 4-2 away to

Barnsley and player-manager Raich Carter left Bly out of the fifth - a home game against Grimsby Town. City had retained the same line-up in those first four matches, but Joe Robinson, Jimmy Greenhalgh and Denis Durham were brought into the line-up for the clash with the Mariners. Bly was axed as Robinson, who had appeared in only eight League games in one-and-a-half seasons following his arrival at Boothferry Park from Blackpool, was given his chance. Bly initially went in the opposite direction because he was sent to play for City Reserves against Grimsby Town Reserves at Blundell Park while the two first teams met at Boothferry Park. Robinson, meanwhile, played in the next seven first-team games, conceding a total of 10 goals and keeping the Tigers' first clean sheet of the season. But in the final game of the sequence City lost 3-1 at home to Leicester City and Bly was recalled the following week - a goalless draw at Chesterfield on Octoner 14, 1950, in which he was badly injured. He was forced to miss the rest of the season and discovered the down side of the game in quick succession by being dropped and then injured on his recall. The outcome was that Bly played in only five first-team games in 1950-51 - comfortably the lowest return of his long stay with the Tigers.

It was to be Bly's longest spell out of City's first team in 14 postwar seasons. Robinson played in 33 of the 42 League games and three FA Cup ties and John Savage, who did not really relish his spell at Boothferry Park with his first League club, deputised on four other occasions - his only senior games for the club.

The second occasion on which Bly was dropped from the first team was in slightly strange circumstances in November 1954. City played a friendly game two days after they had lost 1-0 at home to Bristol Rovers and Bly was rested. He had played in the League game against Rovers, but City manager Bob Jackson decided to choose David Teece for the friendly against a team called the Starlights at Boothferry Park. The Tigers won 7-1 and yet Teece kept his place in the side for the next League game. It was a visit to Blackburn Rovers the following Saturday and City went down 4-0, but Bly missed eight games and Teece enjoyed his longest run in the first team during his spell with the club. There is an ironic sequel to the extent that Teece, in fact, returned to Boothferry Park with Oldham Athletic in April 1958 when they lost 9-0 to the Tigers with Bly in the opposite goal. It remains City's biggest postwar League victory.

But when Bly was dropped for the second time by City during the 1954-55 season, the signs were far more ominous because they finished 19th in the Second Division. And after finishing near the danger zone, they promptly dropped into it the following season and stayed there. The Tigers propped up the Second Division table and conceded a total of 97 goals in the League in 1955-56. It remains their worst postwar defensive record: only in their relegation season 20 years earlier have they ever conceded more - 111.

Bly's season was thrice disrupted by injuries, but he let in 59 of the 97 goals in 26 appearances although he was in goal for their only three clean sheets of what became a topsy-turvy season. They had attracted a gate of more than 20,000 for their first home game of the season and yet there was a crowd of 31,123 for their penultimate one because it was against Leeds United, who were clinching promotion to the First Division with a heavy touch of irony - Carter was their manager. The last home attendance of the season then plummeted to a mere 5,232 as City said goodbye to the Second Division at the opposite end to Leeds.

It was Bly's first experience of relegation almost 20 years after he had joined the club, but it was to happen to him a second time with Bob Brocklebank again at the helm as the manager.

The characteristic yo-yo effect meant that City were relegated in 1959-60 only a season after having been promoted from the new, deregionalised Third Division. But it was also to herald a watershed in Bly's fortunes with the Tigers because it coincided with the third time in which he was dropped from the side and his departure from the club in cold, callous and cruel circumstances.

The 1959-60 season did not start well and in only the second game of the season Bly let in six goals in a League game for only the third time in his career. The first time it happened was away to Sheffield Wednesday: this time it was away to Sheffield United and Bly was injured. City won only two of their first 15 games and Bly let in five goals in a home game - against Lincoln City - for the first time with the club. The game also coincided with the start of Brocklebank's gradual introduction of three experienced forwards - Jackie Sewell, Ralph Gubbins and Roy Shiner - and there was a marginal improvement with three victories in six games. But then the Tigers began to look doomed after winning only once in the 12 League games.

Bly himself had three injury lay-offs during the season and the final one occurred on his 400th League appearance for the club at home to Bristol City. After a five-match absence Bly returned for a 1-0 defeat against Huddersfield Town at Leeds Road on March 12, 1960, and played in City's biggest win of a poor season - 4-0 at home to Stoke City - five days later. On March 26 the Tigers lost 1-0 against Bristol Rovers at Eastville and Brocklebank dropped Bly after the game, which had attracted an attendance of 12,236. Alf Biggs was the last player to score a League goal against Bly, lifting the ball over him from George Petherbridge's pass as he came out. It was reported that Bly produced "good saves after some uncharacteristic handling errors," but it was the end of an era. He was only a few weeks short of his 40th birthday, so it was hardly a convenient time to be left out. As it turned out, it was to be Bly's last appearance in League football. For the third time that season Bernard Fisher took over from him and kept his place for the remaining seven games. City, ironically, remained unbeaten in them, largely because Dave King was given an extended run in the side and scored five goals. But they also gave away just five goals during the sequence.

None of it prevented the Tigers from finishing 21st in the Second Division and enduring relegation with Bristol City. Their biggest problem had been their lack of goals because they scored just 48 - comfortably the lowest tally in the division. City had conceded 76 League goals - plus another five at Fulham in their only excursion into the FA Cup - but it was by no means the worst record in the Second Division. Charlton Athletic had conceded 87 in finishing in seventh position and Swansea Town had given away 84 in finishing in 12th place. Bly had played in half of the Tigers' League games - 21 - and let in 34 of the 76 goals.

City finished two points adrift of Portsmouth, who escaped the drop in 20th spot, and it is a mere matter of conjecture as to whether Billy Bly's future might have turned out differently if they had managed to stay up instead. He had bought a confectionery shop near Boothferry Park and he was contemplating becoming an estate agent, but he said: "If the club offer me terms for next season, then I shall certainly be playing. I am just getting the estate agent's business on its feet, but, like everything else, it takes time and hard work to build up. I feel I must get the business on its feet before I give up football and anyway I enjoy playing."

The warning signs in football, though, were there for him, City pleaded financial difficulties and on April 28, 1960 - two days before the final game of the season at home to Ipswich Town - Brocklebank wrote to him. The main text of the letter contained just 33 words, which read in blue type: "I have to inform you that my directors have decided not to retain your services and have granted you a free transfer. Your service with the club will terminate on June 30 next."

It meant that 23 years of Billy Bly's life had been brought to an end with just 33 words. They were bland, brusque and businesslike words. They contained no trace of feeling, no hint of gratitude and no suggestion of good wishes for the future. Would anybody seriously deny that it was a case of man management at its worst?

It also begged the question as to who had actually sacked Billy Bly as a Hull City footballer. Brocklebank was the manager and he was supposed to be in charge of football matters. That, surely, was his job. Yet he categorically wrote that the decision had been made by the directors. It might, therefore, be safe to assume that there might have been a possibility that Brocklebank had wanted to retain Bly and yet he had been overruled by his board. The real truth may never be known, but, if it were otherwise, why had Brocklebank not had the courage to state that the decision had been his?

At that time there were eight City directors, including the three Needler brothers - Harold, who was the chairman, Henry and John. The board incensed the Hull public with their insensitive handling of their long-time hero. Relegation was bad enough, but the sacking of Billy Bly - and the manner of it - was the last straw for the fans.

The Tigers' home attendances that season did not drop below the 10,000 mark until April 1960, but then there was a gate of 8,691 for a 3-1 win over Swansea and 9,744 for a goalless deaw against Sunderland. City needed all the help that they could get and there was an immediate clamour for Bly to be recalled for the last game at Boothferry Park that season when his departure became public knowledge. The fans demanded one last opportunity to say their farewells to the club's longest-serving player in an appropriate manner. It would not have done any harm because City were already down, it would have been a good public-relations exercise when they desperately needed one and it would have mollified the impact of the decision to release Bly.

The board, though, had already proved their insensitivity and indifference and were unyielding. As a result, City beat Ipswich Town 2-0 in front of a crowd of just 5,719 while Bly was on duty with the reserves at Lincoln. Significantly and pointedly, it was the Tigers' lowest home gate since the last game of the 1955-56 season - against Stoke City - when they had again been relegated from the Second Division. No-one knows for certain if the attendance would have been considerably higher against Ipswich if Bly had been awarded a fitting way of saying goodbye. The signs from the public, though, suggested that it would undoubtedly have been the case. And how many people might have actually stayed away because of the manner of his sacking as much as the club's decline? City, of course, needed friends after a relegation season and yet they did not seem to have much idea of how to win them over and influence them.

The official reasons for their decision to release Bly related to his age. They were that his reflexes might be slower and that his availability might be reduced because of his poor injury record. Bly, in the meantime, largely kept his own counsel in typically-diplomatic fashion, restricting himself to observing: "I would have liked to have completed next season because I intended retiring then anyway." It was noteworthy that he would have equalled the record held by goalkeeper Ted Sagar for the longest service given to one club by one player if he had been allowed to stay on for one more season. Sagar, a Yorkshireman who had played occasionally for England, had been with Everton for 24 years from March 1929 to May 1953 - and had gone to Goodison Park just four months after having had a trial with Hull City! That in itself might, of course, have put a question-mark against the longevity of George Maddison and Billy Bly if Sagar had been taken on by the Tigers. Conversely, what might have happened to Sagar if he had joined City and not displaced Maddison? Would Sagar then have still been around when Bly joined City eight years later? If only...

As it was, Bly was just another name in an uncompromising cull by Brocklebank in the wake of relegation as City struggled to cope with the financial strain of it all. Denis Durham, Bly's long-time colleague and friend who had joined the club in 1947 and also enjoyed two promotion seasons with him, was also freed and joined Bridlington Town. Graham Wilkinson, a defender who had appeared briefly during the 1958-59 promotion campaign, Benny Bridges and David Leveson were also released. And five other players - Colin Smith, Mike Bowering, Jimmy Duncan, Frank Harrison and Jack Bennion - were transfer-listed only a year after having helped the Tigers to promotion.

Brian Taylor, the Hull Daily Mail's venerable soccer writer, summed up the situation as adeptly as ever. He pointed out that Bly had had three benefits with City and suggested that he had had the best treatment possible for his many injuries, but he captured the ground swell of public opinion on the matter perceptively: "Never was that trite phrase 'There's no sentiment in soccer' more apt than when applied to Billy Bly, who, after 23 years' service as Hull City's goalkeeper, was placed on the club's end-of-season, free-transfer list without so much as a thank-you. To the man whose daring and skill have thrilled thousands of soccer fans, a terse, formal note signed by manager Bob Brocklebank was the official notification that the club did not want his services any longer. I do not think that this is the way that Billy Bly should be allowed to fade from the soccer scene. His name has become a household word throughout the East Riding and it has grown synonymous with the name of the club. They have known for some weeks that he was likely to be one of the players who would not be retained and there has been ample time to plan some way to mark the end of his career. I can scarcely believe that the club want to see him out of the game without some tribute. It may be impracticable right now because interest in soccer is already waning. But Billy Bly has made such an impression on everyone's memory that he will not be forgotten by the time that another season comes round and it would be a fine gesture if City promised now that he will not go out of football unnoticed."

The club, meanwhile, rightly and understandably took the flak from the fans about their treatment of Bly with little dissension. There was an immense sense of public outrage and abundant views were expressed in myriad and multifarious manners.

One supporter wrote: "I still find it hard to believe the way Hull City have kicked out Billy Bly. Don't the club want any supporters in the Third Division next season? I, for one, will be half-a-crown a fortnight better off."

Another stated: "Hull City's decision to discard Billy Bly is a shameful action in return for the service and loyalty that he has rendered the club and the game. The board should take heed because their action may mean that they will lose supporters for all time."

Another mused: "I feel thoroughly disgusted by the shameful treatment accorded to Billy Bly, as must thousands of other fans, both in Hull and throughout the country, who have been thrilled by his many wonderful displays during the past 23 years. Whoever is directly responsible for this heartless decision is a matter of conjecture, but to my mind it seems typical of the present attitude of Hull City towards their players. It has destroyed the last morsel of respect I had left for the club. It will certainly take something very startling to attract me to Boothferry Park again next season."

Another insisted: "I read with disgust of the treatment meted out to Billy Bly. I wish him all the best and, like thousands more, say: 'Thank you, Billy, for the entertainment you have given us. I am sorry that the directors have not done their jobs as well as you have done yours because we should have been enjoying First Division football, which they promised us 14 years ago, instead of heading for the Fourth Division.'"

Another declared: "Billy Bly earned Hull City thousands of pounds in gate money in his 23 years with the club. I would like to see Bly and his pals go to Mansfield Town to Raich Carter and show the directors up. 'Good luck, Billy, and thank you for the way you have played so well down the years, taking so many knocks for City.'"

Another maintained: "Hull City are losing more than a goalkeeper in not retaining Billy Bly: they are losing a lot of supporters. Surely there cannot be another club in the country where the loyal are so disdained and the useless so safe."

Another asserted: "It was with deep regret that I read of the decision by Hull City not to retain Billy Bly for another year. It would have at least given him the opportunity to equal Ted Sagar's record at Everton. As one of his many thousands of admirers, I take this opportunity, however, to wish him a successful business life."

Another contended: "Fourteen years ago a handful of men, full of enthusiasm, got together to put Hull on the map in the world of soccer. But there is no progress and financially the club have sunk so low that they try to salvage a few pounds by turning away their most loyal servant, Billy Bly. I believe in tolerance, unity and everything that goes to make life worthwhile and better, but citizens of Hull, shareholders of Hull City, supporters' club members and supporters must all rally round before it is too late and demand the resignation of the board of directors. If they will not resign, will someone go to the next board or shareholders' meeting and give them a talk on how to treat and deal with humanity? Of course, they could still bury their pride and give to their true, genuine and loyal servant Billy Bly the recognition he so truly deserves."

Another avowed: "The kicking-out of Billy Bly by Hull City directors is typical of what has happened before. But a more popular player never wore City's colours. I have read with heart-warming interest of the people who have written about Billy. Does public opinion count for nothing with Hull City directors? I say to the directors: 'Rescind that notice and bring Billy Boy back again.' We the paying public demand it."

Another suggested: "May I add another bouquet for Billy Bly, a courageous entertainer for so long, and a brickbat for Hull City for allowing such a personality to leave the game he has graced without a proper farewell? City could still redeem themselves and possibly save a big drop in gates by reinstating Bly for another season. Alternatively, they could arrange a match to enable Billy to say his goodbye in a manner befitting such a great artist."

Another urged: "I agree about the dismissal of Billy Bly. But could not something more concrete be done to commemorate the great service of the city's outstanding sportsman of the past two decades? There would be no lack of support among the sportsmen Billy has thrilled since the 1930s."

The great Tom Finney, who was known as "the Preston Plumber," was retiring from playing at the same time. He had given 23 years' service to Preston North End although he had been only an amateur with the club between 1937 and 1940 and his send-off from Deepdale provided a timely parallel with the unceremonious treatment handed out to Billy Bly by Hull City.

One City fan wrote: "People can hardly find words to express their views on the treatment of Billy Bly, one of Hull City's greatest goalkeepers. What a difference in the treatment handed out to Tom Finney at Preston! Billy should have been allowed to play in the last game at Boothferry Park so that the supporters could pay their tributes to him."

Another declared: "What a pity it was not possible to place the Hull City directors and management on the free-transfer list instead of Billy Bly, who has given of his best to the club for such a long period! The shabby treatment meted out to him after 23 years' loyal service is a blot on the club's name. What a contrast to the farewell given to another long-serving player, Tom Finney!"

Another commented: "What a contrast - the heartfelt cheers of farewell for Tom Finney and the treatment of Billy Bly! After 23 years of loyal service, surely he could have played as captain on his own ground and in front of his own crowd in his last game."

Another proclaimed: "It is always sad when brilliant and loyal footballers retire. This week English football lost a great forward, Ton Finney, and a great goalkeeper, Billy Bly. It is appalling to compare the gracious retirement accorded to Finney by his grateful club with the scurvy treatment afforded to Bly. As a loyal supporter of Hull City for many years, I am ashamed of the club for the first time. Lack of money is no excuse for lack of courtesy and appreciation. This treatment would be unpardonable if Billy Bly were no longer consistently good, but how many times this season, as in the other 22, has he stood between opposing forwards and a cricket score?"

Another insisted: "Directors of Hull City gave a big insult to Billy Bly in not playing him as captain in what would have been his last home match when the club played Ipswich and an even bigger insult by giving him a free transfer after his long service. I am pleased to see that many City supporters think the same and they are right in saying that Bly deserved the same recognition as that other great player, Tom Finney. I would like to see some token of appreciation for Bly's services from the supporters, who, at any rate, have the intelligence to recognise his ability."

Another announced: "I have never met Billy Bly, but his presence in goal was always assuring to a fan such as myself. I have seen Bly save his side from crushing defeats time and again at great personal risk to life and limb. Like Tom Finney, Bly should have gone out of football with honours."

Another maintained: "I saw the televised report on Tom Finney's last game for Preston. Banners were raised in the huge crowd, who sang: 'For he's a jolly good fellow' - a fitting farewell for a great player. My thoughts then turned to another great player, Billy Bly, who has been a loyal servant to his club for 23 years, almost an all-time record. I would gladly have joined in the chorus and held the banner for him, but I did not fancy singing a solo at Sincil Bank. If this is the way that a club treat the longest-serving player in their history, then I fail to find words to express my disgust."

Another contended: "Allow me to say something that costs nothing and gives great pleasure in the saying. 'Thanks, Billy Bly, for your good service, good sportsmanship and memories.' Our hard-up Hull City have thrown away an extra £1,000 gate money by being either blind or stupid. Maybe the Deepdale reception for that grand player Tom Finney would have been bigger, but it would not have been better."

Similarly, there were fans who also felt that Durham, whose own devotion to the club was never rewarded with a testimonial match, as well as Bly had been treated badly because he was also a long-established player. Accordingly, they suggested that the club's blunt and brusque treatment of their loyal servants was closer to being the rule than the exception.

One supporter wrote: "Hull City directors' treatment of Billy Bly and Denis Durham is just like throwing something into a waste-paper basket. Bly has always been a great goalkeeper and there will never be another like him at Boothferry Park. But he will always be able to hold his head high when he passes any of the directors."

Another commented: "The treatment of our old friend, Billy Bly, has put the lid on a miserable season. The sooner the Hull City directors realise that they have dropped a clanger by their lack of good manners the better because because their treatment of such a long-serving player has really angered the whole of the sporting public in Hull and district. Wherever you go the topic is Billy Bly and, if Hull City want to enjoy any success in the future, the directors will need a different approach to the game. If their treatment of him is any criterion, what future can a player have with a club who show little thought for people such as Bly and Denis Durham? I think that an explanation is required from the directors as to why Bly and Durham were not asked to play in the final game because supporters are really bitter about the whole affair and many people will stay away next season."

Another insisted: "How much longer are the soccer-loving public of Hull going to stand for the set-up at Boothferry Park? Is it not plain that City have lost all touch with the public - if it ever existed? It would take a very poor board indeed to have ushered out Billy Bly and Denis Durham in a worse way than the present one did."

Durham himself remained philosophical about the treatment handed out to him and Billy: "Everyone felt down that season, but, as always, people have to cope, so we did. There was a fighting spirit in the team that made us lift ourselves to fight on. Being released was expected before too long because I was nearly 37 and Bill was older. We knew it would be only a matter of time because the body won't work as well at that age and I played only a handful of games for Bridlington Town afterwards."

At any rate City's board panicked under the immense weight of adverse criticism about the way in which they had sacked Bly in particular and called a Press briefing - a rare occurrence in those days - to try to take the sting out of the situation and rescue their own tainted credibility because Sportsmen Say, the Hull Daily Mail's sports letters column, had been inundated with complaints about the affair. The Press conference was conducted by chairman Harold Needler, vice-chairman Ron Buttery and Brocklebank and was even attended by Bly himself as City turned out their big guns to try to defend their action.

Needler said that the club would have liked Bly to play on for a further season, but they were in such desperate financial straits that they could not have afforded to have kept him. And he added cryptically that several players had been retained after the 1958-59 promotion season as a mark of the board's appreciation when they might have been transferred in different circumstances. He also insisted: "As far as the club are concerned, there has never been a wrong word between us and Billy in all his 23 years' loyal service. If only we had had 11 Billy Blys, the lives of we football-club directors would have been made much easier." At that time their lives might have been more bearable if they had handled Bly's departure with dignity and diplomacy.

Buttery, who had been a director of the old Hull City when Bly had first joined the club, claimed that there had always been long faces in the boardroom when City were deprived of Bly's services because of injury. But he added that Bly must have been satisfied with his treatment from the club because he had never handed in a transfer request.

On the subject of whether Bly should have been selected for the last game of the season against Ipswich after having been told that he was being released, Buttery conceded: "If the team for that game were being picked this week, then Billy would certainly be in it." Unfortunately, his opinion was at odds with Brocklebank, who indicated - after Needler had passed the buck to him - that the side had been more successful in the closing weeks of the season and he had wanted to encourage them to maintain their improvement by leaving their complement as intact as possible.

But the supporters had also been enraged by the fact that Bly was not only omitted from the first team against Ipswich, but he was also forced to play for the reserves in the North Regional League the same day. Three days earlier they had also packed him off to Workington with the reserves. This time he led them against a strong Lincoln City Reserves side who won 6-1 at Sincil Bank in front of a crowd of about 1,400. And although Bly captained City Reserves that afternoon, it was still something of a demeaning way for him to play his last competitive game for the club after 23 years.

The public agreed because one fan wrote: "No doubt I am only one of many wishing to register a protest about Hull City's treatment of that loyal and faithful servant Billy Bly. I think that it is absolutely shocking that he was allowed to bow out of the game he has served so well for so many years by playing in the reserves. I can think only that it was lack of thought and downright bad manners on the part of the board of directors. City will be one supporter less next season."

Another added: "I have been a keen supporter for many years, seeing them on every possible occasion whether they were winning or losing, but never have I been more disgusted than with the treatment doled out to Billy Bly. To play him in the reserves in his last match with the club instead of letting the few regulars still left at Boothferry Park give him the cheer he so richly deserves is, to my mind, nothing short of an insult. Bly is still a great goalkeeper and deserves some acknowledgement of his long service to the club."

Another insisted: "Of all the shabby treatment possible to mete out to a player, that given to Billy Bly, Hull City's long-serving and able goalkeeper, is the most atrocious. He played his last game in the reserves yet the first team had nothing to lose or gain. This confirms my oft-repeated statement that Boothferry Park is a graveyard for players and managers alike."

Another maintained: "I have supported Hull City for 12 years, but I shall never go to Boothferry Park again - not even if they should reach the top of the First Division - because I am absolutely disgusted by the way in which the directors have sacked Billy Bly. The least they could have done was to allow him to play his last game in the first team at Boothferry Park, where City fans have idolised him for 23 years."

As to the terse brevity of the letter informing Bly about his sacking, Brocklebank claimed at the Press conference that he had just been conforming to FA standards in its formality. In addition, Needler and Buttery strenuously denied that there had been a feeling among the board that Bly was a bad clubman. They all seemed to protest too much and the need to try to give explanations showed that they had misjudged the mood of the public, were out of touch with the fans and had been unable to treat a loyal servant with at least a semblance of compassion and understanding.

They tried to atone for their errors of judgment by promising to arrange a floodlit East Riding Invitation Trophy game the following season when the proceeds would be divided between Bly and the East Riding County Football Association. Bly himself commented: "I have made a lot of friends and I want to thank the directors for what they are doing for me with this match." He whimsically added that he would hope to play in it - if he were not injured!

The Tigers had first played in the first East Riding Invitation Trophy in May 1947 and they had become regular friendly games - sometimes on a two-legged basis - until October 1958. City's opponents had been varied and comprised Grimsby Town, Barnsley, Sunderland, East Fife, York City and Hibernian. The truth of the matter, though, is that they never played in another game in the competition - they played in no friendlies at all from January 1960 to March 1963 - so the club's pledge to Bly was not kept.

But one director, Bob Metcalfe, did resign from the board in a protest about the general running of the club, especially the financial aspects of it. Oddly enough, he had also had a special rapport with Billy because he lived down Westella Road, Kirkella, and regularly used to throw sumptuous garden parties. And his star turn at them was a display of goalkeeping skills by Billy...

In the meantime, Bly himself was immediately in demand locally after City had announced his departure and a few days later he played as a guest for Bridlington Town in a charity game against the Green Howards at Queensgate. It was jointly in aid of the Green Howards' Benevolent Fund and the World Refugee Year Fund and the game attracted a crowd of almost 1,000. Town won 2-1 and Bly was reunited with some of his old Boothferry Park teammates because Bob Dennison captained them and Mike Head and Benny Bridges, another guest, scored their goals.

Furthermore, Goole Town held their annual dinner dance at the town's Station Hotel in early May amid a certain amount of speculation that they might try to sign Bly because there was a body of opinion that they would attract a lot of Hull's soccer public to their games if they did. The president of Town's supporters' club, Ald. Fred Gosney, insisted: "The way Hull City have allowed Bly to leave means that half the sporting population of Hull will not be going to Boothferry Park again. I can visualise Goole making a sensational signing, which will result in Bly coming to the club with many Hull supporters." They also felt handily placed to move in for him because their manager Martin Reagan, who later took charge of the England women's team, had played alongside Bly for the Tigers in 1947 and 1948, but it never happened.

All it demonstrated was the public esteem and fondness for Bly and the spontaneity and intensity of the fans' protests made sure that City's reputation was severely tarnished because of their handling of his departure. In fact, the way in which it happened set a trend because the only three other players to have since played more games for the club than Bly did - Chris Chilton, Andy Davidson and Garreth Roberts - were all meted out unsatisfactory treatment of their own when it became time for them to move on. Chilton moved on to Coventry City after one of the directors had mistakenly addressed him as "Ken," Davidson was sacked as assistant manager in 1979 after having served the club in playing and backroom capacities for 31 years and Roberts was initially invited to stay on with the club as youth coach before the offer was then withdrawn a few days later. By and large, it seems, the Tigers did not treat their long-established, loyal servants too well.

The public reaction and show of admiration towards him brought some consolation to Bly, who also had to deal with the death of his 79-year-old father, William, at 132 Wharrier Street,

Walker, on May 16. His widow, Annie, helped by her eldest son, Ernest, left her bungalow in the North-East after being encouraged to go south and moved into a home in the Bournemouth area, close to other members of the family.

It was naturally a very difficult phase for Billy, but he had support from his public and it was amply demonstrated by local woodcarver Cyril Hurst, who taught a group of youngsters from the Hardwick Street area of Hull how to make a foot-high figure that might be presented to him. The accompanying letter read: "This is a small token of our appreciation for your wonderful service to Hull City in particular and football in general."

Bly himself was always remarkably undemonstrative about his sacking by Hull City, but Bernard Fisher, who replaced him as their first-choice goalkeeper, recalled: "When it was announced that he was leaving, it was a little surprising, but again I think it was more to do with club finances, so nothing changes. He was released with some other players, but on reflection I'm sure that they should have given him one more season. The news broke just as all the players dispersed for the summer, so we had no time to talk about it. I can't remember Billy saying much about it, but I feel sure that he was most upset."

Billy, of course, rarely allowed his emotions to get the better of him and accepted it all in gentlemanly fashion, but his son, Roy, reflected: "It was something that he never spoke to me about. I was always round the house at the time and I can remember it, but I was only 10. I just know that it was the darkest time for him. I don't really know how he felt, but I can't imagine how he carried it all.

"Funnily enough, we never ever discussed it because my dad never looked back in that sense. Over the years we never talked about the past too much. It all never came out, but my dad had given Hull City a lot of service over the years and what they did was an awful thing to do to anybody. Knowing my dad as I did, he would have wanted to get round the table and discuss things rather than to be told that his reactions were slower and it was time to move in a new direction.

"It was the bland, curt way in which it was done. It was no action of gentlemen or a board of directors in the true sense. I know that it was a very bitter experience for my dad even though he didn't come out with anything directly. Maybe it had been time for him to go, but it was just the way in which it was done."

9

All the Way to Weymouth

Billy Bly's final contract with Hull City expired on June 30, 1960. Unless he then decided to continue in top-class football at the age of 40, he was now relegated to the role of shopkeeper and would-be estate agent. Time was not on his side in football and in reality the offers were not likely to come flooding in. When City released him, he said that he might have been interested in playing for another League club within easy reach of home on the understanding that he could train at Boothferry Park. But he stressed that he had absolutely no intention of going into non-League football.

The public did not quickly forget him and the controversial manner of his departure from Hull City. There was, in fact, a delightful cameo in May 1961 shortly after Bob Brocklebank had resigned as City's manager before moving almost immediately to Bradford City. While there was still a managerial vacancy at Boothferry Park, one correspondent wrote to the Hull Daily Mail's Sportsmen Say column: "The manager of Hull City has resigned officially 'in the best interests of the club.' Now is the chance for the directors to show to Billy Bly some appreciation of his 23 years' service to the club by asking him to be manager. I have not heard of anything that has been given to Mr. Bly, so the supporters would appreciate this gesture by the directors."

In reality, it had been extremely unlikely that Bly would play on at anything other than local level and that is what he eventually did because he joined East Hull side Brunswick Institute, little knowing that out of the blue another option might be just round the corner. But his declaration that he would not be interested in playing in the higher and wider echelons of non-League proved to be inaccurate.

He suddenly found himself busy in the autumn of 1961 because he had to contemplate one final appearance at Boothferry Park. It was the one so callously denied him by the board at the end of the 1959-60 season, but it did not come in League football. It came instead in his own testimonial match on October 19, 1961.

Bly's City teammates testify to a story that he told them about the origins of the game. He had apparently asked for a testimonial match in recognition of his long service, but club officials had told him that the Football League had turned down the directors' request on his behalf. Bly, though, privately told some of his colleagues that he had by chance met Alan Hardaker, the Hull-born secretary of the Football League, on a train journey and had politely asked why the application for his testimonial match had been rejected. Hardaker, it seems, replied that the reason was very simple - the League had not, in fact, received one in the first place. It would then appear that a combination of a touch of guilt and a spirit of compromise might have culminated in Bly being belatedly awarded a testimonial game 18 months after he had been informed of his release.

Roy Bly certainly got the impression that the circumstances surrounding the testimonial match were unsatisfactory in various aspects. It did not really prove to be the opportunity for the Hull public to pay due tribute to one of their favourite footballers of all time because he observed: "Something somewhere happened. I have heard it said that he even had to organise his own stewards for his own testimonial match and that the club gave him one date for it - one choice only."

Even then Hull City did not provide their current players for the game and Billy turned out for his last farewell to Boothferry Park as a player alongside a group of his former teammates instead. He had to scramble around of his own accord to find players to take part in the game and Bernard Fisher, his fellow City goalkeeper, recalled: "I remember going with him to a match at Bolton in a Rover car he had then because we were arranging for players for his testimonial game. That night the rain was horrendous and it pleased him that I map-read."

The match programme, costing sixpence, did not contain any form of tribute to Bly or gratitude for his services from the board. Instead his contribution was lauded in articles by Brian Taylor, the Hull Daily Mail's soccer correspondent, and Cliff Britton, City's new manager.

Bly himself wrote a vote of thanks: "Tonight is an occasion I will always treasure even though my heart is heavy with the thoughts of bidding au revoir to football. Through the generosity of the directors of Hull City I am provided with this opportunity of saying a big thanks to you the public for all your encouragement, sportsmanship and tolerance towards me throughout the years. Every footballer needs these to support him and I ask you to give the same help to my successors and indeed to every player.

"It has been my pleasure to play before you and I hope you have enjoyed watching my efforts. I find it difficult to express my feelings in words, but I can simply say that my career with Hull City has been extremely happy, both with the management and my colleagues past and present. I would like to express my sincere thanks to the directors, the manager, secretary and trainers."

But the weather was poor and a polio epidemic was engulfing Hull, so the attendance was remarkably disappointing. It amounted to just 5,387, a lot less than many of the crowds in front of whom Bly had played in his hey-day, and it brought him just £600 for his long service.

Bly played behind his old teammates, such as Wilf Hassall, Denis Durham, Bill Harris, Trevor Porteous, Jimmy Greenhalgh, Ken Harrison, Stan Mortensen, Norman Moore, Bill Bradbury and Brian Cripsey. The opposition, known as the All-Stars, included illustrious names such as Tom Finney and Billy Liddell and it was entirely appropriate that their goalkeeper should be Bert Trautmann, who suffered one of the most famous goalkeeping injuries of all time when he broke his neck and yet played bravely on for Manchester City to help them to beat Birmingham City in the 1956 FA Cup final at Wembley. The Ex-Tigers won 4-3 and, entirely fittingly, Bly pulled off a wonderful point-blank save in the last minute to ensure his side's victory.

Billy had also played for singer Ronnie Hilton's Showbix XI and it was just as well that he got himself a touch of match practice - albeit in a friendly environment - in his testimonial match because he was to receive an offer to return to higher-grade soccer. It was not to be a comeback at League level, but it was close to being the next best thing. And it might well have not happened if Britton had not succeeded Brocklebank as City's manager.

Weymouth, then in the Premier Division of what was known at the time as the Southern League, were managed by Frank O'Farrell, the former Republic of Ireland international who was to take charge of Manchester United 10 years later. As a player, O'Farrell, a wing-half who was originally from Cork, made his name primarily with West Ham United, but in the latter part of the 1950s he moved to Preston North End and the manager who took him to Deepdale was Britton. He went on to replace Brocklebank at Boothferry Park in July 1961 and the following autumn O'Farrell, by then Weymouth's player-manager, renewed his acquaintance with one of his old mentors. He needed a goalkeeper in an emergency in time for the second round of the FA Cup and wondered if Britton could help him out in any way.

Billy had continued to train twice a week since leaving the Tigers and he had applied to the FA to become a permit player - an ex-professional who turned amateur - with local club Brunswick Institute. But Weymouth stepped in on the recommendation of Britton and Billy said: "I have trained with the lads at Brunswick Institute and had decided to apply for a permit to play for them. Now the FA have to defer my application until after the cuptie." Perhaps Billy was lacking confidence for once because it was going to be after three cupties and for the rest of the season.

O'Farrell had started to telephone round because his first-choice goalkeeper Bob Charles had broken his arm badly in the first round of the FA Cup when Weymouth beat Barnet, then a top Athenian League side, 1-0 at home. He recalled: "I had joined Weymouth as player-manager for the 1961-62 season after spending four-and-a-half years as a player with Preston North End. Nearly halfway through the season Bob Charles, a young goalkeeper who had been signed from Arsenal, broke his arm and it meant that both our goalkeepers were injured at the same time. I was desperate, so I decided to ring Cliff Britton, who was manager of Hull City at the time and had been my manager at Preston. I rang him to ask if knew of any goalkeeper he could recommend to help me out in the emergency.

"He mentioned Billy Bly. He did say that he was 41 years of age, but he said that he had played in his own testimonial match shortly before my 'phone call. Cliff said that Billy had done very well, but he didn't know how he would react to travelling all the way down to Weymouth to play because it was almost 300 miles from Hull. But Cliff said: 'If he'd come, he'd do you a good turn.' I spoke to Billy, explained the problem that I had and was half-expecting him to turn me down, knowing the distance involved, so I was delighted when he did show an interest and said he wouldn't mind at all."

Billy's reaction to the situation was simple and predictable and typified his kindly demeanour towards lending a helping hand in a crisis: "I know what it is like when you are a man short. Frank O'Farrell was in a bit of a fix and most other goalkeepers are cuptied, so I had no hesitation in making up my mind to help out."

O'Farrell got a pleasant surprise and Roy Bly recalled: "Dad kept himself pretty well fit, but Frank thought that nobody in his right mind would go on a 300-mile trip to play for him just at the weekend. But dad answered the SOS, he met Frank at King's Cross and signed for Weymouth in a tearoom there. He stayed with my auntie down at Parkstone, near Poole.

"Frank used to say that he was a bit concerned at the start that dad would be there on time. But they'd give him details and he'd be there half-an-hour before the team 'bus every time. And his training sparked something in the part-timers at Weymouth. The team seemed to lift themselves, so the story goes, so that they performed so well in those cup matches. The motivation seemed to have been: 'If that old so-and-so can do it, then so can I.' They put extra effort in and got their rewards."

O'Farrell added: "I knew of Billy's playing history with Hull City, of course. He was a very fine goalkeeper and he had been unlucky, in many respects, with injuries. He probably could have got higher honours if he had not been a bit unlucky with injuries and had not been playing for Hull City, who were not in the top echelon of clubs at that time. But he was a very fine professional and he had a great reputation as a player and a person.

"We agreed to meet in the tearoom at King's Cross station in London. He would travel down from Hull and I would travel up from Weymouth. I explained that I needed a goalkeeper until the end of the season because of the predicament with having my other two injured. When I met him, I was very impressed with him because he was obviously a good professional and a good person. My immediate impressions of the man were very good indeed. I put the proposition to him and said that I thought that he would do the job that I wanted, to which he said that he would be happy to come down and play.

"He said that his son, Roy, had kept a diary of his games in a scrapbook as proof of his career. But he said that, when he had retired from the game, the scrapbook had been closed because there wouldn't be anything more to put in it. When he signed for Weymouth, though, he said: 'I'll have to tell Roy that he'll have to open up the scrapbook again because there might be a bit more to put in it!' Subsequently there was. Another thing I remember him saying to me at the time when he signed was that he would bring me luck. He said that he wasn't very lucky for himself, but that he brought other people luck. And I said that I hoped that he'd bring me luck and that he'd also be lucky this time.

"I explained to him that I would like him to come down on a Friday for home games and that was no problem. And if we were going to staying overnight for away games, then I'd also expect him to be there on the Friday. Then, when we would be playing away at places such as King's Lynn, Bedford Town, Cambridge United or some of the Kent clubs, I would have to be confident that he would be there when we got to the ground on the Saturday, but he always was. When we got to the ground on a Saturday, I'd look out for his car and it would be there - I think he drove a Rover at the time - because he was very reliable and a first-class professional. Anyway we agreed the deal and he signed.

"Sometimes we would have two matches at home in a week, but then he would stay over rather than travel all the way back up to Hull and come down again. I think he stayed with a relative in the Bournemouth area and, if he did that, he would go to where he was staying and then he'd come back in the following morning and do some training. He was just a good professional. He'd do his exercises and get the medicine ball out. Of course, this impressed the other players who saw him do it. They trained at night two or three times a week because they were part-time professionals.

"He played, but funnily enough the reaction to him wasn't great. The local Press asked why I had gone away and signed a 41-year-old goalkeeper, but I was always a believer that age didn't matter. If a man were fit and could play, it didn't matter what age he was. Very often 41-year-old good professionals were better than 21-year-olds who were not such good professionals."

Ironically, Weymouth already had a readymade link with East Yorkshire in their midst because their squad included Ken Bryan, who had been born and brought up at Hedon, near Hull. In fact, he played for Bridlington Town in the 1960s on his return to the East Riding, but then went back to the South Coast to live at Portland, near Weymouth.

Bryan remembered: "I supported Hull City when I was a youngster in Hedon and Billy Bly was my hero, so it was unbelievable to meet him eventually during his time at Weymouth. I was a member of the side that season until two weeks before Billy came, but I was unable to play because I'd cracked an ankle bone playing at Guildford."

Billy also lodged with a lady called Eileen Gray in Newstead Road, Weymouth, as well as staying with family in Parkstone and soon adjusted to his change of surroundings. He had a warm-up with some of his new teammates on the old Weymouth Recreation Ground, for example, and said: "That was just what I needed to get the feel of the ball. Now I am ready. But I must have at least one game before the Cup because I don't want to let Weymouth down."

Billy made his debut for Weymouth in a 5-1 win at home to Wellington Town on November 11, 1961. He was armed with a good-luck telegram from the injured Bob Charles and local sports supporter Bert Hicks recalled his impact: "I was in the large crowd when Billy first turned out for Weymouth. The atmosphere was electric. They just had to win and they did - and it was all down to Billy Bly in goal."

Weymouth also had a league game away to King's Lynn before the FA Cup tie at home to Newport County, then struggling in the old Third Division, on November 25. Billy, happy to be a wanted man again, relished the prospect and said: "I've had hundreds of thrills out of soccer, but none greater than this one." Furthermore, John Lloyd, of the Daily Express, wrote to him on November 20: "Like everyone in Fleet Street, I'd like to see Billy Bly make a triumphant return to FA Cup action. And I have a feeling that the headlines after the match will be: 'Bly, Bly, Newport!'"

Ironically, Hull City had won 2-0 against Newport, who were managed by former Scottish international Bobby Evans, at Somerton Park a week before the cuptie and Billy was allowed to train at Boothferry Park in the build-up to the cuptie. Accordingly, he gleaned some information about Newport from his some of his old teammates and O'Farrell admitted: "Billy learned some very useful things. I think they should help us."

It was enough to turn Weymouth into giant-killers as they beat Newport 1-0 at home with an 87th-minute goal by Colin Court. An added bonus was that Roy Bly was allowed to be Weymouth's mascot for the tie and he recalled: "My memory is that I went down with my dad for what was an amazing occasion for a child. I didn't see much of the game because I was so small. For some reason, I didn't make myself known to the right people to get to the dug-out, so I was on tiptoe on the other side of the fence with all the supporters and didn't see a great deal of it.

"But on the way back we travelled by train and stayed at the Great Northern Hotel at King's Cross. We went from Weymouth to Waterloo in an old style of carriage with candlesticks on the tables and we had a meal, at which wine was served although I was on orange juice. Then we went into the station buffet at Waterloo and I was put in a corner while I continued to have orange juice and crisps, as you do at that kind of age. My father never had beer, but he liked a tot of whisky.

"On that journey back Frank O'Farrell, my dad and Southampton's Terry Paine, who later played for England and happened to be on the same train, never stopped talking football. Come midnight on the Saturday, my father had had a few whiskies and probably a couple of glasses of wine. He always said that he wouldn't have made it on his own and was grateful that I could make out which way to go and which tube stations to go to so that we could get to King's Cross. I was at a tender age of 12 and he always used to have a laugh about how I got him back home and could remember where we were staying."

Hull City had been knocked out of the FA Cup at the second-round stage when they lost at home to former manager Bob Brocklebank's Bradford City, so there was never a possibility that they might be drawn against Weymouth. Billy, therefore, said that he wanted Weymouth to draw Manchester United in the third round "because they beat Hull only by a disputed goal

12 years ago." After all, he had not had the chance to seek revenge for that defeat because he had been injured when City had beaten them 2-0 at Old Trafford in the third round in 1951-52. It was further ironic because United were later managed by O'Farrell, but Weymouth were not to earn themselves a plum draw at all.

O'Farrell recalled: "When we got to the third round proper, there were three non-League clubs left in the competition - King's Lynn, Morecambe and Weymouth. At that time the draw was broadcast on BBC radio at 12 o'clock. Most people had the habit of getting round a radio and listening for the draw. We did likewise and were in the boardroom down at Weymouth. There were the directors, the staff and myself listening and hoping, of course, that we would be drawn against a big club.

"King's Lynn came out early and they were drawn away to Everton, which was a good draw for them because they would get a big gate and enjoy their day. We were hoping that we would be drawn against another big club and that the same thing would happen to us. As it happened, the draw came out as Morecambe versus Weymouth. It was so unbelievable that there were two non-League clubs drawn against one another in the third round of the FA Cup. It was going to be pretty much a disaster for whoever were going to lose after they had got so far. To be drawn against another non-League club with a small gate meant that there was nothing at the end of it. It was a bit hard for the clubs to be drawn that way, but we went up to Morecambe and won 1-0."

The third round on January 6, 1962, had brought a reunion for O'Farrell because Morecambe's player-manager Joe Dunn had been one of his teammates at Preston. Weymouth now hoped that they would get a good draw in the fourth round on January 27 and this time it was going to be even more special for O'Farrell in terms of a reunion.

He recalled: "We again hoped that we would draw one of the big clubs. King's Lynn had been knocked out by then, so we were the last non-League club left in the competition. Again on the Monday we were all sitting round the radio and hoping for a big club and a big gate so that we could enjoy our day out, give a good account of ourselves and bring back some money.

"As it was, we were drawn away to Preston North End, who were the club I'd left at the beginning of that season to take over as player-manager of Weymouth. Of course, they weren't the biggest-supported club in football. They never commanded more than 25,000 to 27,000 gates, so there was a bit of a disappointment again."

The tie was hardly a disappointment to Roy Bly, though, because he was invited to be Weymouth's mascot again and Billy reflected: "Roy is thrilled about going to Preston. He has already told his pals at school that he will be at Wembley this season. Roy's first experience of being team mascot was in the second-round home clash with Newport. He led the team out and had the cheek to try a few shots at his old man while we were warming up, but he didn't beat me! We had a tough game, but eventually got through 1-0 and the board gave Roy the mascot's rig-out as a souvenir."

What Billy thought of training sessions in preparation for the cuptie at Deepdale is not recorded, but Weymouth's pitch was so wet that the players trained on the promenade, where extra lighting was supplied! But the tie was at least to produce one of the funniest incidents of Billy Bly's career.

O'Farrell recalled: "We went up on the Friday and we had to get permission for the lads, who included a carpenter, a postman, a plumber and a schoolteacher, to be off work. We stayed at Blackpool and on the Saturday we took the coach to Deepdale at Preston. It was a bit foggy

Blackpool and on the Saturday we took the coach to Deepdale at Preston. It was a bit foggy along the way and it was still quite foggy when we got to Deepdale, but anyway we went into the ground, the gates were opened and the crowd were coming in. We got changed and went out to play, but I was surprised really that the referee started the game because I honestly couldn't see both goals when I was tossing the coin in the middle of the park.

"Anyway we started off the match and I remember that I had about two throw-ins and a couple of kicks of the ball, but you lost sight of it when it went a certain distance away and you didn't know where it was until it came within reach of you again. After 13 minutes the referee blew his whistle, called us together and said: 'Look, it's very bad, so we'll go off the pitch for a while, go into the dressing-rooms and see if it'll clear up.' An announcement was made over the tannoy about what action he was taking, so all the players went into the drying-room to keep warm until such time that it had improved to resume the game.

"There were 18,000 people at the match that day - not a big gate, but a reasonable one. But all of a sudden somebody noticed that Billy wasn't with us. Somebody said: 'Where's Billy Bly? He must be still out on the park.' Somebody else suggested that someone had better go out and look for him. I can't remember who went out, but he found Billy still in the goalmouth and he didn't know that the referee had taken us all off the park. It showed how poor the visibility was. When he came in, I think I asked him: 'Billy, what were you doing out there? We've all been in here for a few minutes.' He said: 'I didn't know. I thought you had them under pressure up the other end!' It was so funny because everybody were killing themselves laughing. It's quite a funny story, but a true one."

In fact, Weymouth's trainer Sammy McGowan was the one-man search party sent out to bring Billy in from the fog and Roy Bly also remembered the incident with great amusement: "I was really chuffed to go because I was Weymouth's mascot again. It was an amazing occasion when the fog came down. It was foggy when we were kicking about before the game, but it started. And then they took the players off the pitch after a while. I went in to the boiler-room with the players to keep warm. We sat down in there, but everybody had come off the pitch except my father. He was still between his goalposts waiting for the ball! Somebody in the boiler-room said after about 10 minutes: 'Where's Billy?' Everybody looked round and someone said to me: 'Where's your dad?' I said: 'He must still be on the pitch.' I hadn't realised because it was packed in there, so they sent out for him."

The cuptie could not be resumed because of the fog and it was agreed that the two sides would try again two days later. O'Farrell said: "The referee didn't resume the game, the fog never lifted and both clubs agreed to play it again on the Monday night, so we went back to Blackpool and I had to ring the players' bosses and tell them what had happened."

This time, though, Weymouth were to be without their mascot because Roy added: "My dad had to go and meet the Weymouth team for the actual game when it was replayed, but I wouldn't go because I loved my football by then and I had a match of my own for my Sunday team, Eastfield Boys, which was important to me. Looking back, though, it would have been a good experience to have gone back to Preston."

The abandonment had at least meant that Weymouth were still in the bag for the fifth-round draw earlier in the day on the Monday and they or Preston were drawn to meet Liverpool, whose manager Bill Shankly was at the replayed tie. But North End, for whom Shankly had played as a wing-half, ensured that Weymouth were unable to indulge in any more giant-killing.

O'Farrell remembered: "It was a lovely evening on the Monday and we gave a good account of ourselves, but we lost 2-0. Alex Dawson scored one and Peter Thompson, who eventually went to Liverpool and was being watched by Bill Shankly that night, got the other. There had been 18,000 there on the Saturday and there were 27,000 there on the Monday night, so we had an aggregate of about 45,000 people. They never got their money back on the Saturday, so in the end those two games were the equivalent of being drawn against a big club over one game. We came out of it with a lot of credit, most people were impressed with our performance and we took some money back with us as well.

"In that game Billy played with a broken finger. It had been fractured in one of the previous games, but we didn't highlight the fact that he was injured. At the time there was a journalist called Laurie Pignon, who used to write for the Daily Mail and he was very good to us during our cup run. He gave us some publicity and would write something every week about us.

"But I didn't want to tell anybody that Billy had a broken finger because I didn't want the opposition to know that it was painful and that it had had to be strapped up. But after the game I mentioned that Billy Bly had played a number of games with a broken finger and Laurie Pignon was quite upset about it. He felt that I should have told him so that he could have written about it before the match, but my job was not to give something away that might have been an advantage for the opposition, so he took exception that I hadn't given him the news which he wanted to write about and, from being very friendly towards us, he got a bit shirty about it. But that's the way it was, it was my decision and I think that that was the right thing to do for the club."

Billy, though, made the most of his extra time in the FA Cup in a big game at Preston and Jack Wood wrote in the Daily Mail: "When the final curtain came down on one of soccer's greatest stories, the youngsters who had watched him bound through this last 90 minutes rightly picked out Billy Bly as their hero. Forget that 41-year-old Bly had a hand in Preston's first goal and remember that for the rest of the game he did things of which a goalkeeper half his age would have been proud because he made great saves from Alex Dawson, Peter Thompson and Alf Biggs. The goals that beat the former Hull City star came just before and after halftime, but at all other times he was the complete master of Preston's fiery, hard-shooting forwards."

It had been announced during the build-up to the Preston tie that Weymouth were planning to apply for Football League membership and the immediate question concerned the possibility of whether Bly, who had originally been signed for the duration of the Cup run, would confirm that he would be willing to extend his stay until the end of the season. Club chairman Reg Bartlett said: "It is really up to Frank O'Farrell. If he wants Billy Bly to continue, then I don't think the directors will stand in his way." Bly, who was a £15-a-week part-timer on month-to-month contracts, replied: "There is nothing I would like better. It's great to be back in the game in this way and I have enjoyed every minute with Weymouth."

Former Stirling Albion goalkeeper John Boyd was due to start a month's trial with the club, but he damaged his hand in an Army game, so talks between O'Farrell and Bly began before the cuptie at Preston. O'Farrell, who was so impressed that Bly had been prepared to travel between Hull and Weymouth twice a week just for the sheer joy of playing, said at the time: "He is tremendously enthusiastic and a great example to the younger players. He has done a magnificent job - not just on the field, but by his enthusiastic example to the youngsters off it. This week he has stayed in the town and I have had to stop him from training at times otherwise he would have been at it morning, afternoon and evening every day. But that is the kind of man he is and the kind of man we want around." Weymouth's reserve goalkeeper Dick Whitson even took two days off work to be coached by Billy and O'Farrell added: "It should have done Dick a great deal of good and will come in handy in the future."

Bly helped Weymouth to finish sixth in a division including Oxford United, Cambridge United, Cheltenham Town and Hereford United, all of whom were to become Football League clubs, and O'Farrell, who stayed at the club until the autumn of 1963, reflected: "Billy played until the end of the season and I think we had a reasonably good run. But then he went back to resume normal life again after the interruption down at Weymouth. I always said to people that Billy Bly was one of the nicest persons I ever met in football. He was a really nice guy and I was very fond of him. I had great respect for his ability and he was a lovely person. He was genuine, he was a nice person and it was a privilege to have known him. I always speak in the highest terms about him, his experience at Weymouth, my dealings with him and what he did. Later on I was delighted to see him when I went up to Hull as manager of Torquay United. I know he was a credit to the game and I know that he was a credit to Hull City because of the years that he gave to them.

"While Billy didn't achieve the same honours as Tom Finney, he was still spoken about in the same terms. I still see Tom, Tommy Thompson and Willie Cunningham because we have an ex-Preston North End association and we meet for a golf day and a couple of other functions each year. They were great players and Billy was a great player, but they earned very little from the game in comparison with the present-day stars. But they had something else that many present-day players haven't got - they had a love for the game, they respected the game, they respected the opposition and they were all on the same wage. None of them earned more than £20 a week because that was the maximum wage. That was probably the wage that Billy was on when he retired from Hull City.

"He was one of that rare group of players at that time whom people still talk about with respect. That's the greatest thing that you can have - the respect of your fellow professionals and the respect of people who go and watch you and see you perform to the best of your ability week after week and year after year. Billy was a one-club man and that's worth more than money. I wonder how many of today's players will be remembered by people who follow football in the same way as Tom Finney and Billy Bly. It was a pleasure to have met Billy and he was lucky for me as he said he would be. And I think that I brought him a bit of luck as well because he enjoyed being in the game a little bit longer and he enjoyed his time at Weymouth. He was back in the spotlight again as a result of the club having an FA Cup run and performing against Preston North End in the fourth round.

"They were good memories and I think that I'm a better person for having met Billy. I was delighted that I was able to bring him a little bit more luck than he thought he'd had before that. We stayed good friends and it was a pleasure to have known him. It was an unforgettable experience and I always mention Billy Bly when I talk about people I liked very much. During my career Billy Bly was one of those players who was at the top of my list."

Billy's exploits with Weymouth had hardly been an embarrassment for Hull City, but he had unexpectedly had a belated opportunity to exorcise the ghost of his badly-handled departure from Boothferry Park and he had seized it with both goalkeeping hands. And Roy Bly admitted: "There was a desire on my dad's part to prove a point to Hull City when he signed for Weymouth - not outright, but subconsciously. I would have reacted in the same way. If you're worth your salt, you'll show people what you're worth in a different way if you get the opportunity.

"It was also a time for him to extend his career as a goalkeeper and a player. He had the opportunity, he loved the game and he didn't think about anything else other than: 'Yes, I'll do it - even though it means travelling all those miles.' He wanted to do it for himself and it was an opportunity that he couldn't turn down, but maybe he wanted it to serve as a reminder to Hull City - maybe so. He was always philosophical about such things. His attitude was: 'Here's an opportunity which has come to me. I'll take it.' He was asked, it extended his love for the game and he wouldn't have any reason to say anything other than 'Yes' to it.

"And even though Frank O'Farrell was surprised that my dad took his chance because of the travelling involved, my dad's love of the game overrode it. The desire was still there even though he was a bit older than most, but the experience was there as well. He knew he could do a job for a short period of time because he was still very fit, but he also might have wanted to send a personal message privately to those who spoiled his time at Hull City. Going to Weymouth was a good experience and I think that, if he hadn't have taken it and grasped the opportunity, then he wouldn't have known what would have happened. It's the same with everything in life."

10

Family Man

Billy Bly might have been a model professional as a footballer, but another aspect of his life was also of paramount importance to him - his family. He enjoyed a long career in soccer, but his commitments to those who were nearest and dearest to him were never very far away from his thoughts and considerations.

A life in football does, out of necessity, bring its own special commitments and working hours, but Billy always ensured that it did not interfere unduly with his family life. He worked round his family and always spent time with them. He did not relish being away from them and always tried to retain contact with them wherever he might be as part of his soccer calling.

Billy's upbringing in Newcastle made him well aware of family values. His childhood as part of a big family had been tough at times, but he came from an era when people accepted their lot, rarely complained and made the best of what they had. Such a background set out parameters and standards and the beliefs ingrained in Billy from his early days never left him. In other words, he had become aware of what was needed to become a doting, dutiful family man long before he had a family of his own. After all, he had been born in 1920 just after one world conflict and was embarking on building a family of his own just after another.

Billy married Dorothy Norma Scott, whose father, Robert, had been a plater's keeper in the Tyneside shipyards, in July 1943. But, according to their son, Roy, it might never have happened: "The story that my mum told me was that there had been a foursome on a date and somehow it got twisted round, so my dad ended up going out with Dorothy when his mate had originally been supposed to go out with her."

Billy retained a firm sense of proportion about the importance of his family life as soon as he and Dorothy were married and that approach shone through during the latter part of the Second World War. He often preferred to spend time with Dorothy rather than to play football when opportunities arose and Roy, in fact, always believed that Billy's stance on family matters did not go down well with FA secretary Stanley Rous, who was knighted in 1949 for his services to the game. Rous was responsible for placing players on leave to clubs during the war years and Roy has always wondered if Billy's reluctance to turn out on every available occasion may have counted against him later in his soccer career in terms of receiving greater international recognition.

He reflected: "Going back to the war years, my dad did say to me that when he got leave from the Army to come home from wherever he was stationed, he would much rather see my mum because it lasted only 24 or 48 hours. A lot of players guested for other clubs, as my dad did at times, but he used to turn down games as well. He would not play in every game in which he was asked to play because there weren't that many hours available when he was home on leave and he often chose to see my mum instead.

"And Stanley Rous used to be involved somewhere in the system of allocating games for professional players, but dad probably turned down more games than he played and he always felt that it held him back in terms of his selection and his career, possibly at representative level. He just felt that there was an influence working against him later. And I just have a feeling from conversations with my dad that his standpoint didn't go down too well with some of the football people. My dad didn't say so outright, but I formed an opinion from what he did tell me that that might have been the case although it was one of those stories that never really came out of the cupboard."

Billy and Dorothy soon had their first child - a daughter called Norma, who followed in her father's footsteps in one sense by being born at 150 Church Street, Walker. When Norma, who was given her mother's middle name, was about 18 months old, she and Dorothy came to Hull once it became clear that Billy could still pursue his career in professional football. Dorothy had her own strong sense of duty and was quite happy to stand by her man as he set about establishing himself as a goalkeeper when the dust settled on the grimness of the Second World War.

Dorothy, in fact, quickly adjusted to life in East Yorkshire and later recalled: "I loved the place and the atmosphere. I thought it was great and settled very well indeed." Billy, for his part, was well aware that he had been away a lot in the early part of his marriage because of his Army service and that he was embarking again on a footballer's existence that, out of necessity, also brought plenty of travelling and time spent away from home. He had always tried to keep in touch with Dorothy during the War and was even photographed in his bedroom while writing home to her from Hanover in 1946. And he maintained the same philosophy during his football career: it even included a classic instance when he was away from home in England.

Towards the end of the 1947-48 season City took their players away early in preparation for their three-game Easter programme, which began with visits to New Brighton and Oldham Athletic in successive days. The Tigers took a party of 15 to Southport, where they had twice stayed earlier in the season, and they arrived three days before their opening Easter game on the Good Friday, March 26. They had previously beaten Southport in the FA Cup's third round and received a civic greeting in the town, but this time Billy was missing home. And on March 24 he sent a postcard of Southport Pier to Dorothy, in which he reported: "I am having a nice time. The weather is lovely and I hope it is the same for you. Look after yourself. See you soon."

More significantly, he would regularly send her postcards from City's club tours. They showed the importance of his family to him and, although they were not borne out of any homesickness, they were sent on almost a daily basis on some occasions.

When the Tigers visited Scandinavia for an end-of-season tour in 1948, for example, he sent six cards to Dorothy from Denmark and Sweden. Initially they were posted between the friendlies against a Jutland XI in Aarhus and a Kolding XI.

The first, showing a photograph of the radio headquarters in Aarhus, was sent on May 9 after the Jutland game and Billy wrote: "Just got back from playing and enjoyed it, but we were lucky to get away with a draw 1-1. They got their goal with a spot-kick. I am all right, so don't worry. The weather is lovely here."

The second showed the Himmelbjerget and Billy wrote on May 11 as soon as the City party had had their dinner after their arrival in Kolding from Aarhus: "On this card is the place where we got off the boats, walked up the hill to the top and we could see all round the country. It was lovely and we got the buses back to Aarhus from there."

His next card of Kolding explained: "We arrived at Kolding at 11.30 this morning. We have been up to the ground, doing a bit of training this afternoon. I may play tomorrow. Weather is lovely."

Alec Corbett, in fact, was in goal for the Tigers' 5-1 defeat by a Kolding XI and on May 13

Billy sent a postcard showing the town centre to Dorothy: "We have all been round the slaughter and bacon-curing factory this morning. It is another fine day here and I hope it is as nice at home. I think I will need a rest when I get home, dear. I hope the garden is all right. We leave for Copenhagen in the morning and arrive there at 4.30. Alec stopped a spot-kick last night and our lads were beaten 5-1. Alec had a good game: so did all the lads. We're off to Copenhagen!"

On reaching Copenhagen with the City party, he wrote: "We arrived at Denmark's airport at nine last night. It was lovely. It was just like being on a bus."

The Tigers moved on from Denmark to Sweden for the final leg of their tour, drawing 2-2 at Malmo FF when Billy shared the goalkeeping duties with Corbett after starting the game. And he wrote home: "We arrived at Malmo in Sweden at two o'clock today. This place is lovely. I wish we had been stopping in Sweden longer and had more money. I have got something for you and Norma. I think you will like them. I hope you and Norma are keeping fit and well."

The comment about money is intriguing because Billy kept the tour schedule issued by City director Stanley Kershaw. It shows that he withdrew a total of £6. 14s. 8d. in Danish and Swedish currency and was informed: "Your next wage packet will have this amount deducted."

City celebrated winning the Third Division North championship in 1948-49 by going on a four-match trip to Ireland at the end of the season when Billy and Joe Robinson took it in turns in goal, both having two outings. Billy sent a postcard of Belfast City Hall to Dorothy, who was by then expecting Roy, on May 19, 1949. It was after the first match of the tour against Belfast Distillery and just before City's goalless draw with Portadown and he wrote: "Just a card to let you know how we came on in our game. We won 5-3, it was a good game and everybody enjoyed it. We went to the races yesterday, but we won nothing. We are playing tonight, but Joe's playing and then we are off south after the game. We arrive at Dublin at two in the morning."

Billy again retained the tour schedule when the Tigers visited Israel and then Turkey in May 1950. Kershaw's instructions included: "It is estimated that it will be very pleasant and warm in Palestine and the temperature, as in Turkey, is equal to that of London in July. The main thing is to have light shirts and changes of socks, but no overcoats or heavy clothes are necessary." The party travelled by train to London on May 9 and flew out to Rome from Northolt Aerodrome by Skymaster the following morning. They spent a day in Italy before moving on to Tel Aviv.

Billy also sent regular messages back to his parents, William and Annie, in Walker and his first postcard to them was sent from Italy: "Just a card to let you know we have started our tour. We left London yesterday at three o'clock and arrived at Rome last night at 11.30. All we had time for was supper and bed. They are taking us around Rome before we go because we leave here at 12 o'clock and we have 10 hours in the air. The weather here is lovely. I hope pop got home all right and I hope you and pop are keeping well."

There followed a postcard of Ben Jehuda Road in Tel Aviv and Billy wrote: "Just a line with a view of Tel Aviv and to let you know I will drop you a letter tomorrow. We left Rome at one o'clock yesterday and we arrived at six o'clcock in Turkey. We left there at 10 o'clock and arrived in Tel Aviv at three o'clock this morning. It was four by the time I got to bed. I am keeping fit and well. Hope you're all the same."

On another occasion he wrote: "Just a card from Jerusalem of David's Tower. I wish you could have seen it. We have had a good look round all the places, but it would be too hot out here for you. The heat is getting us down."

The Tigers played Hapoel Tel Aviv and an Israel XI on the first stage of the trip - Robinson was in goal for both games - and Billy also wrote home to Dorothy: "Just a line to let you know I have been to Jerusalem. We had a good look round all the old places, but I was disappointed because they wouldn't let us go into the room where the Last Supper was. I hope you are all keeping well because I am in the pink."

City then moved on to Turkey to play games against Adana Demispor and then Glencerbirliji and Billy, who played in them both, wrote to his parents from Ankara in the first instance on May 22: "Just a card to let you know we are leaving Ankara for Istanbul by train tonight at nine o'clock. We have played two games and we won 4-0 and 3-1. The last game was worse and I am pleased we are finished here. We may play Sunderland in Istanbul and that is our last game. Hope you're keeping as well as I am."

The clash with Sunderland, who had originally travelled with City's party, never materialised and the following day Billy wrote again to "ma and pop." The postcard read: "Just to let you know that we have just arrived in Istanbul. I hope you are all in the pink as I am and I will be pleased to get back home again. You can't beat England. This view is what you see when you look out of the front of the hotel. I will close now with all my love."

Billy also sent a message home to Dorothy: "Just to let you know that we arrived in Istanbul about an hour ago. I was looking forward to a letter, but you must have your hands full or you would have sent me one. This is what you see from the front of the hotel. I will close now and send you a letter later."

The 1950-51 campaign was difficult because of Billy's longest injury lay-off, but he devotedly sent cards to Dorothy, who was then staying at Long Benton in Newcastle, from the Tigers' end-of-season trip to Spain. The first was sent on May 23, 1951, en route from Paris and showed the Theatre de l'Opera: "We left Manchester at 2.30 and we arrived in Paris at 5.20. We stop here for an hour and then on to Barcelona. I hope you and the kiddies arrived home safe and sure. I will drop you a card when we get to Barcelona. Weather okay: hope the same for you."

On arrival, he sent a postcard from Sitges, just south of Barcelona, to Dorothy in Long Benton, in which he reported: "We arrived in Barcelona at 11.30 last night and had tea at the airport. We left at 1.30, arrived at this seaside place at two o'clock and it was raining. The weather is very nice, but there is a strong wind blowing. We are spending much of our time here while in Spain, so we will be in the sea most of the time. We have had a game of golf today. I hope you are all keeping well."

City were based in Sitges, but another postcard was sent on May 25, the day after Billy had played in a defeat against Atletico Madrid: "We are now in Madrid and we leave tomorrow at two o'clock. We played last night and lost 4-0. The better team won because our lads had a very bad game, but I will tell you about it in a letter from our next place. I'm having a job to get a red bag for Norma. Hope you, Norma and Roy are keeping well."

Billy again sent postcards to his parents, the first of which was sent from Sitges. It showed the local beach, adjusted some of the timings in one of the cards to Dorothy and read: "Having a nice time. Left Hull for Manchester at 9am and arrived 12.30. Had lunch and left by air at 1.30 for Paris. Arrived there at 5.30, left Paris at 6.15 and arrived at Barcelona at 11.30. Had some tea, left by bus at 1.30 and arrived at this seaside place at three o'clock. It was raining when we arrived here, but it is lovely today and we have had a game of golf. Most of our time will be spent here, so we will be doing a lot of swimming and sun-bathing. Hope you and pop are keeping well. Letter to come."

Another followed the lines of the one sent to Dorothy and said: "We are now in Madrid and it is a lovely city. We played last night and lost 4-0. The better team won and our lads played badly. Hope you and pop are keeping well. I have got something for pop and I will get yours tonight. I am having a nice time."

City also lost 2-0 to Atletic Bilbao before Billy was recalled in place of Robinson for a game against a Barcelona XI that brought a 5-3 defeat, but the regularity of the postcards from various venues throughout his career show his devotion to his family. He was always one for knowing that he had a job to do wherever it took him, but he never forgot the folks back home.

Billy, in fact, had started to make his mark as a sporting hero by the time that Roy was born in a Cottingham nursing home on September 2, 1949. He was named after Billy's brother Roy, who had tragically died within a few days of being born, and there was immediate speculation as to whether another potential professional footballer had arrived on the scene. Billy played in a 3-3 draw at home to Bradford City the day after Roy's birth and the subject was broached there and then, but he just replied: "We shall have to wait and see how he goes on."

It was a philosophical, diplomatic reaction and Billy remained phlegmatic about the prospects much later on because Roy said: "I think my dad tended to protect me from football. We never got into depth about any subject really. On a Friday night before home games I used to keep him in line beforehand because we used to go off to the Carlton cinema together. I used to look forward to it. We'd have discussions, but he certainly wouldn't go into too much detail and he certainly wouldn't push me one way or another in terms of my career.

"He'd say: 'This is what I do, but, if you find that you are good enough in anything that you do and you want to do it, then do it. But don't do something because I do it. Do it because you want to do it.' If it had been football, that was fine, but that was it. It didn't have to be. There was no pressure at all. In some respects I think that perhaps we would have benefited a little by covering one or two aspects of the game more. But we used to talk about the enjoyment of it more than the real side of the professional game. I was protected from that and never knew much about what happened.

"He never pushed me to play football or to become a goalkeeper. He just let things progress naturally. In later years he once said to me: 'Whatever you do, I'll always be proud of you. If you want to go and play football, go and do it. But whatever you do, always do it to the best of your ability.' That stuck with me and always came naturally to me. I've always given 100 per cent."

The outcome was that Roy developed his own interest in football later rather than sooner. It happened in his own time in his own way and it happened naturally without any undue parental pressure or expectation. Roy added: "I can recall that, from about the age of 10, I was more aware of what my dad did, but in a strange way. And, because of his popularity, I found that I was shy when faced with any publicity or any group of people. I was very proud, but I was quiet and reserved. Like my dad, I just liked to get on with things without too much fuss.

"I was 10 before I was interested in football, but I went quite often to see him play towards the back end of his career with Hull City. I would go behind Bunker's Hill and stand behind his goal. But in those days you could walk all the way round the ground, so I used to go and stand behind his goal for the whole match, whichever one he was in. You could get a transfer to the other end of the ground, but most people would go round to be behind the goal that City were attacking, but I was a defender and dad was a goalkeeper, so I'd stand behind the one that he was in!"

Dorothy and Norma also went to Boothferry Park to watch Billy in action and Roy added: "My mum was always there to support him and went to a fair few games, but not a lot when I was younger because she was always looking after me and I didn't start going until I was about 10." Norma, who now lives in Lincoln, supported the Tigers when she was growing up in Hull and can recall visiting Boothferry Park from an early age herself: "My mum would put me in my pram and take me down to matches from Worcester Road. When I was older I would go down to Boothferry Park on my bicycle and the office staff used to look after me during matches."

Norma also recalled a special trip to the ground when she was a promising athlete: "Dad used to take me to training when I was with Hull Harriers and bring me back. But on one occasion he even took me to Boothferry Park so that I could train there."

Roy, meanwhile, gradually came to terms with Billy's lifestyle as a professional footballer as he grew up. His own interest in playing soccer developed as he started to understand what it all meant and he could put it all into its proper context: "As a boy of four or five years of age, I gathered that my father was a good painter and decorator and I could get round that one. But I also recognised that he went off and played football. I was often asked by mum and dad: 'Do you want to come to the football?' But between the ages of five and 10 I was, like most kids of today, better off playing on my own in my own mind, so I preferred to stay at home or go to the Priory cinema. I'd even go to a matinee when they used to have yo-yo competitions.

"But one day our group at Eastfield School were asked if we'd like to play football and organise a team, so something was sparked off. My dad got home from training one day and I suddenly surprised him by saying: 'I want to have a go at football, but I need some boots by tomorrow dinnertime.' Nothing was too much trouble for dad and, sure as anything, I had a pair of boots for the following day.

"I always remember that, when I got my first football boots, my dad made me stand in a bucket of cold water in them one leg at a time for 20 minutes or so to soften up the leather. Then they would have to dry out naturally. I had to stand in the bucket in my boots with my football socks and shinpads on, but he told me that the idea of it was that the boots would start to mould to the shape of my feet.

"He also showed me how to nail in the studs, which we had to do in those days. My dad had gained previous experience because one of the skills that he'd picked up in the Army was as a cobbler. He'd do any little cobbling or stitching jobs. He'd be mending boots and there'd always be a last in the garage at home. He'd take me in there and show me how to take old studs out and put new ones in. He often mended shoes and soccer boots and at times he would also do hand-stitching for people because he could repair anything that was leather in terms of stitching."

Billy also had an expertise in carpentry and his woodwork, in which he dabbled as a hobby, was highlighted during the build-up to the FA Cup quarter-final tie at home to Manchester United in 1948-49. In one pen picture, it was insisted: "He likes making tables and wooden toys in his spare time."

Billy was also an enthusiastic gardener and Roy recalled: "My father used to spend long hours digging the garden and planting his vegetables, such as potatoes. The garden went a long way back in Worcester Road and he used to love spending lots of hours there. It was his way of getting on with things. That's how the days were filled out then - doing jobs around the house and garden."

The garden, though, once caused a moment of concern about Norma for the rest of the family when she strayed into it one day because she said: "I can remember going into dad's vegetable garden, picking all his beetroot and eating it. I got into trouble from dad because I was wearing a white dress at the time and it made such a mess. At first everyone thought that something much worse had happened to me!"

Billy did not play professional soccer in an era when there was a lot of money to be made out of it and he had to adapt to family life as everybody recovered from the austerity of the War. There was rationing for a spell and in those days people were grateful, above all, that peace had returned after the horrors of the world conflict and materialistc matters were of secondary import. Roy recalled: "Things weren't great and we had things, such as chairs and a settee, that probably should have been taken to the tip rather than put inside your house. But there wasn't a lot of money around for people settling down after the War. Our first television when we were at dad's shop was black-and-white although he did get a motor car when we were down Worcester Road in a club house. It was a Morris 8."

If there were comparatively little money to be spent, there was still time to be spent with the family and Billy readily accepted his parental responsibilities. Norma described her father as "strong and gentle with academic qualities" and Roy recalled his devotion to his children: "Dad was a really caring person. He was unbelievable at times. He'd look after us, encourage us and take us all over. He did spend time with us and used to love taking us to the parks - Pickering Park, West Park or even East Park, where we'd go on the water chute. And he'd often take us to the pictures or gatherings of family and friends. We were disciplined and it was just foreign to us to be anything else. He didn't have to discipline us. He spent as much as time as he could with us although obviously he did tend to be away an awful lot, while mum used to do everything around the house and make everything work for us. Both of them were very easy-going, but you knew your place and we had discipline."

Billy and his family had several other City players in the neighbourhood when they lived in their club house at Worcester Road, but they largely kept themselves to themselves even though they might all travel to Boothferry Park together on match days. Roy said: "One thing I do remember was that there didn't seem to be a lot of knocking about with the other players. There might have been a little bit of socialising, but they were there as teammates. There were quite a few players round about in the club houses, but I can't remember families getting together. If we're talking about the 1940s and 1950s just after the War, things just developed, but it was a gradual process."

But Billy was always polite and sociable and felt a particular allegiance with the fans who supported him so keenly. It was a rapport that gradually developed and then remained. It made him extremely popular with his public and earned him a respect that lasted long after he had left Hull City. And it was intensified when he bought his shop near Boothferry Park. Billy was never remote or discourteous and the purchase of the shop turned him even more into a goalkeeper of the people.

Roy remembered: "There weren't so many commercial possibilities around in those days, but he just loved to perform and do his job. When something such as professional football becomes your job, you don't necessarily do it for the love every day. It becomes a job more than a sport and I think that's how my dad looked at it. I'm sure that there was a lot that went on that the public didn't see, hear or understand, but, from the supporters' point of view, he used to relish it and get a big thrill from meeting people. Dad just handled the public adoration very naturally and didn't show any pressure at all. He just gave me the impression that it was a delight to meet fans and do presentations and that sort of thing. He used to go down to training an hour early and he'd often be the last to get away because he used to get stopped by waiting fans wanting autographs and he never wanted to let anyone down. He never refused anyone.

"I think he might have been a bit homesick for Newcastle as a teenager when he first came down to Hull on the train for a trial, but he soon settled in. He loved Hull because he was with the club throughout his League playing career. He also loved the people and the public and he made some very good friends out of people who were just fans. There were people who would come into his shop, which was open from 8am to 9pm, to enjoy a chat and there were always the people who lived nearby. One couple, Fred and Eileen Nottingham, moved from Airmyn Avenue near the ground to Thornwick Avenue in Willerby, which is where we went, and became family friends.

"Dad got the shop while he was still playing and the lettering that you could see over it was all his own work because he was a signwriter from his days as a painter and decorator. It had a sign saying 'Hull City goalkeeper' and he just added the 'ex' when he retired.

"And he used to love it especially when City got good crowds. And when we lived in the neighbourhood around Boothferry Park, residents would look after the fans' bicycles while matches were on or open their garages and charge about six old pennies for them to park their cars in them."

Like so many people of his generation, Billy Bly had to cope with a lot as he grew up. Life could be both bleak and harsh at times, but it enabled him to rationalise everything and retain an inner calm. He had an unruffled temperament and demeanour and he quickly put everything into perspective. There were no airs and graces: instead he remained down-to-earth and approachable. He set his standards and he quietly and efficiently put them into practice as a parent and a family man. By and large he preferred to keep his emotions in check, but he was nobody's fool. He had a quiet resolve and he was no pushover as a person or a goalkeeper.

Roy reflected: "In general my dad would keep things to himself and think about them rather than react instantly. He would digest things and think them through first. I think I'm pretty well a similar character to him in that respect. But if there were no need to think things through because it was a plain black-and-white situation, then he would let his views be known directly. For example, there was the game against Falkirk when his money was docked: he reacted instantly and rightly so.

"As a father and a goalkeeper, I don't think that he could lose his temper. He would be very firm, but he would be polite. He would have a strong conversation with people round him, but he wouldn't cause a scene and I think that was why he was highly-respected. He was a wonderful man in the way that he used to conduct himself."

11

Later Years

Billy Bly tended to prove that variety was the spice of life when he returned home after his soccer adventure with Weymouth. It kept him in the limelight a little longer although it was something that he never ostentatiously craved and he returned to Hull to get on with his life in trademark fashion - quietly with a minimum of fuss. He still continued to follow his football interests in a low-key way at local level and he tried several business options.

But the Hull public who had idolised him as a goalkeeper never forgot him. He was treated with respect wherever he went and his popularity never waned. Billy remained in demand and he was invited to various functions and prizegivings even though he was no longer in the lime-light with Hull City. In August 1960 he was invited to open the annual home encouragement show at North Frodingham and took Roy with him. In July 1962 he was invited to open Withernsea Tennis Club's gala and this time he took Norma. On one occasion he was asked by the Hull Daily Mail to hand over the £700 prize to Lilian Riby, the winner of their weekly Find-the-Ball competition, in East Hull. He accepted a request to hand over the awards to Blundell Street junior boys' football team in Hull and in December 1972 - more than 10 years after he had left the Tigers - he handed over the trophies for everything from billiards to darts to dominoes at City Engraving Social Club's presentation evening at Hull's C. D. Holmes Club.

In football terms, though, Billy returned to Brunswick Institute. Plans for him to join them for the 1961-62 season had had to be abandoned when the opportunity to play for Weymouth cropped up. Brunswick had mentioned the possibility of Billy taking over as their player-manager as they sought to establish themselves in Yorkshire League soccer, but it was never going to be a realistic idea. He was concentrating on business - he still had his shop near Boothferry Park and he was learning about estate agencies - and he had played few games, preferring to turn out on charity occasions for Hull singer Ronnie Hilton's Showbiz XI. Basically Billy did not want the responsibility of running Brunswick, but, typically, he still offered to do as much as he could, saying: "I am going to help them all I can in building a team and I have told them that it will suit me if I can enjoy a game or two with them."

As it was, the Weymouth adventure had temporarily prevented him from fulfilling his good intentions as he stayed with them until the end of the 1961-62 season. In the meantime, Brunswick appointed Wilf Hassall as their new manager in the spring of 1962. Hassall had played for Hull City from August 1946 to the summer of 1953 although he missed the 1948-49 promotion season because of injury and naturally knew Billy well because of their time together at Boothferry Park. And it was not long before Billy and Hassall, who had had a successful period in charge of Bridlington Town's reserves, were reunited at Sutton Ings.

Towards the end of the 1961-62 season Billy finally turned out for Brunswick in strange circumstances. His debut was not in a league game but in the Brunswick Invitation Cup, a competition which had been inaugurated in 1960. And Brunswick won 1-0 against an East Riding County FA XI after including Bly in their side while their regular goalkeeper, Les Urwin, played for the opposition!

It was intended to be all change for the 1962-63 season because Brunswick Institute were renamed Hull Brunswick and Bly was to be their first-choice goalkeeper as well as Hassall's No. 2. He played in a pre-season friendly at home to Goole Town, which Brunswick lost 4-3, but then disaster struck on August 25. Billy's injury jinx struck again when he broke his arm in a 1-1 draw at Ossett Town and he did not play in another league game until they entertained South Kirkby the following April. Ironically, though, Bly and Hassall did play for the Ex-Tigers that season - against Brunswick, who had Urwin in their goal on this occasion!

Bly stayed on with Brunswick when his close friend Harold Meens, another former City colleague, took over as manager for the 1964-65 season and stayed in charge for 15 months. Billy eventually took over as Brunswick's junior-team manager and in January 1966 he was presented with a badge and then a blazer for his services by club chairman Jim Sellers, watched by gala princess Susan Bratley.

At that stage Billy was still doing work as a painter and decorator after having sold his shop near Boothferry Park. It had been a popular feature when he had bought it early in 1958 and his wife, Dorothy, commented: "The fans used to come into our shop all the time to discuss the matches." But they sold it in the early part of 1962 and moved from the premises at 33 Boothferry Road to a house at 14 Thornwick Avenue, Willerby.

Billy had hoped to merge running his shop and becoming an estate agent when his League career in soccer ended with Hull City, but his plans did not come to fruition and he entered a relatively-quiet phase in his life during the 1960s. Roy Bly recalled: "I think my dad found it hard to adjust in that period after he had finished football. I think that the way that Hull City had treated him had had an effect. It wasn't very courteous in the way it was done."

As a consequence, Billy dabbled in various business projects, but it was only when he went to work at Everthorpe Borstal, 15 miles west of Hull, that he became settled again. Roy added: "An estate agent called Richard Emslie persuaded him to work for him, but things didn't work out even though dad had thought it would give him some useful experience.

"We also had a neighbour called Alec Ramshaw who had been in insurance and then become an estate agent in Anlaby. Dad used to do the sign-writing for his 'For sale' signs because in those days they were made in wood and then painted by hand, so he used to earn a little bit of money doing that in-between. Dad also used to paint and decorate some of the houses on the books, but I think that a lot of people thought that he became an estate agent in his own right.

"Dad also knew businessman Malcolm Healey, who had Status Discount, and he got a job doing time-and-motion painting for him. It got him by for a while, but I don't think he was really settled. Then he got the job at Everthorpe Borstal and he really did love his time there. He worked there for 12 years until he passed away and went as a painter and decorator, but he also taught the inmates it as their trade. They used to get a lot out of him. But not only that, he would go round decorating the prison warders' houses. It was his job, but he got to know the community and the people and he took part in the functions at the social club."

When Billy went to Everthorpe in February 1970, he was reunited with one of his old City teammates, Dave Fraser, who remembered: "When Bill joined us at Everthorpe, I was a senior prison officer. He settled in straightaway, he was always available and he was a genuine celebrity, helping and encouraging officers and inmates. He went about chatting to everybody and it was brilliant because he was so popular."

Arthur Hardy is the manager of the works department at what is now Everthorpe Youth Custody Centre. He went there in October 1971 and recalled: "Everyone loved Billy. I remember particularly how skilful he was at his trade. A large part of our job was helping to pass on skills to those inmates we identified as being able to benefit, become employable and not re-commit crimes once they left the borstal. Billy would obtain Old Holborn tobacco tins and, when time allowed, he would first paint the lids white all over. He would then trace, chalk and draw the inmates' chosen soccer club badges over the impressions on to the lids. It was done skilfully by tracing and hand-painting on to the tins and people were amazed by the results, but they obtained the attention and respect of the inmates. And years later I used the technique I'd learned from Billy to create a 5ft. x 4ft. Manchester United badge on my son's bedroom wall!"

Billy's communications skills in the tough environment of a borstal were also valuable because Arthur recalled: "During one particular period an inmate caused all sorts of problems every time I went on duty. I cannot remember the lad's name, but it must have happened a good 40 times and I had to put him on report to the governor on each occasion. It was a nightmare, but eventually this individual was out with Billy for three weeks and afterwards he was as good as gold. The lad liked football and he followed Billy like a lapdog. But Billy was able to handle people and situations, so he told him stories, gave him advice and enabled him to pick up some skills."

Some of Billy's handiwork and craftsmanship remain at Everthorpe to this day because Arthur said: "The officers' mess is an old Victorian house. At one point it needed decorating, so a group of of us, including Billy, went about the job. The ceiling has a moulded plaster design on it and Billy lovingly painted the grapes and the grapevines. The mess has had restoration and decorating since, but the grapes and the vines have not been repainted - only washed - and people still admire the work today."

Billy got on so well with his colleagues that they were not afraid to play practical jokes on him and Arthur recalled: "Our lockers had moulded fronts and one day we turned Billy's around. We drilled a new keyhole in it and Billy couldn't understand why he couldn't open it with his key. As he tried to get it open, he swore and swore. No-one had ever heard Billy swear before, but he was effing and blinding while we were there having a laugh about it."

Soon after starting work at Everthorpe, Billy helped to establish the Ex-Tigers' Association. Comprised of former Hull City players, they were interested in becoming involved in different kinds of local charity work and he duly attended the inaugural meeting at the social club at Boothferry Park on August 24, 1971. Colin Smith, one of Billy's teammates during the 1958-59 promotion season, was elected as the association's first chairman in his absence and remembered: "I served on the committee with Bill at the start, so we mixed a lot socially. Early on we played together for the Ex-Tigers to raise money for a kidney machine and everything fell into place from that."

Roy Bly, in fact, recalled playing in the opposing team to his father on one of his appearances for the Ex-Tigers. The game took place at Hodgson's Recreation Ground in Beverley on May 13, 1973, to celebrate the East Riding Schools' FA's silver jubilee and Roy said: "Dad wasn't a fitness fanatic in his later years. He didn't go off and play squash or badminton and he put some weight on when he played in amateur football, but he still played in some charity matches and he remained reasonably fit into his late 40s. On one occasion I played against him when he turned out for the Ex-Tigers in a game against a team made up of East Riding Schoolboys at Beverley and I played alongside people such as John Hart and David Lill. But I didn't score against him!"

In the meantime, Roy, who had followed in his father's footsteps when he had a short spell as a player at Hull Brunswick, had joined local club North Ferriby United. It was the signal for Billy himself to become involved and follow Roy, who explained: "Dad went on to the committee and started to help Ferriby out when I played for them. I used to go down to Hull City two nights a week for training and hoped that something might happen for me at professional level, but it never did although I did also go to Leeds United for a trial when Don Revie was in charge. But my dad joined me when I went to Ferriby, where he eventually assisted Mike Rawding when he was manager there. But he was also on the committee and, being a painter and decorator, he used his trade to help out in any way he could. At that time there was no clubhouse down near the pitch, so we'd use the cricket pavilion. But the committee got two old prefabs from the East Riding County Council and the supporters, local tradesmen and the committee members all mucked in as we started to build a clubhouse and dad used to do the painting and decorating. He had gone down to support my playing career as a parent, but he couldn't resist helping out."

Mike Rawding reflected that it was a thoroughly-enjoyable experience for him when he and Billy were the management team at Ferriby from 1972 to 1977: "All the time that Billy was with me during the 1970s it was a partnership. I was the manager with a coaching badge and he was an ex-professional with bags of experience from a long and distinguished playing career. But not once did he make life difficult for me or try to take charge. In fact, he was always most supportive, especially when things were not going well. I remember when we lost four of the first six games at the start of one season and 'the natives were getting restless.' The problem was that I had always selected the same side and it would have been so easy to panic and make changes although we had played the opposition off the park in all the games. We sat down and discussed the situation and decided to write out our team for the next game independently. We both wrote: 'No change' and then we went 20-plus games undefeated.

"On one occasion the opposition arrived late because their coach had broken down and the kick-off was delayed for 40 minutes. But the information came to us so late that all our players had changed and were ready to play, so keeping them in the dressing-room was not an option. Billy said that he would keep them amused and told the players to go on to the field. I went out a few minutes later to see Billy standing in a goal, saving shots from all angles from the edge of the penalty area. The only ones he ignored were low down in the corner of the goal, but, as the frustration of the players grew by the second because of their inability to beat him, few went into that area. It made everyone realise what a class act he must have been in his playing days and the players held him in even higher esteem.

"He had a calmness about him that transferred to others. He taught me that you didn't think clearly when you were het up and in our early days together he was always reminding me to keep my composure. Halftime talks were just that - talks. There was no throwing of teacups or screaming and swearing whatever the state of the game - just a composed attempt to improve matters for the second half. Billy had the confidence of the players and would talk to them individually, offering a bit of advice here and there, and you could see the positive effect that it had on them."

Rawding also talked about Billy's objectivity when Roy was ever left out of the side. Even though the decision affected his own son, Billy never declared his interest as a parent and merely backed his manager's judgement.

Billy remained active on Ferriby's committee as the 1970s wore on. The club had sought new blood and Billy fitted the bill perfectly because he helped out in various capacities in addition to the football side. In October 1976, for example, he helped to organise a sponsored walk to raise money to go towards United's clubhouse fund. He also more or less became the club's official painter and in November 1979 he reported to the committee that all the painting work on the clubhouse had been completed.

Rawding added: "Billy was part and parcel of the club and would do anything to help from painting dressing-rooms to giving players rubdowns before games. I spent several Sundays working with him on the Ferriby clubhouse when it was being built, but he was not impressed with my constructional skills, often telling me: 'You're in the way again, so go and help Ken Alexander to cut the grass!'"

It was also at this time that out of the blue Billy did a very good turn for Hull City. They had just taken on a 16-year-old apprentice forward from the North-East called Brian Marwood and he was struggling to settle in the area. But help was at hand and Marwood recalled: "I first met Billy at an Ex-Tigers cricket match, I'd been down to Northamptonshire before choosing football in preference to cricket for a career and we just got involved in a conversation about sport. We just got chatting and I think I mentioned that I wasn't having an easy time in my digs. When I first came to Hull, Eddie Hamilton and I had been in digs together and it was unsettling. We were on the verge of going back to the North-East, but Billy was very sympathetic and invited us to stay with him.

"Eddie got very homesick and eventually went home, I had found it equally as unsettling at first and most definitely there was a chance that I might have done the same, so it was a fantastic gesture on Billy's part. It helped me because I was in a strange city and it was my first experience of living away from home. It was a crucial time for me and I became very settled because it felt like home at Billy's and I like to think that it made the difference between what I achieved and what might otherwise have happened because it was my first year as an apprentice.

"Billy was working at Everthorpe, but he tried to make time to get to some games and in the evenings we'd chat a lot about football. It was extremely interesting, he was a huge help and in my second year I think I made great strides, as did players such as Garreth Roberts and Steve McClaren. Billy was always calm and collected, he rarely raised his voice and he was a perfect gentleman. I was determined to stick it out and I did so because of Billy and his wife, Dorothy. They didn't have to take somebody under their own roof at their stage of life and feed and water them and look after them, so I am eternally grateful for what they did. Billy and I talked and talked and he made me realise about the whole work ethic, that I should not doubt my ability and to remember that there was a reason why I was there. He helped me to rationalise things, to focus on what it took to be a professional footballer and to think about extra training. Everything Billy said made common-sense and it worked for me."

Marwood went on to play briefly for England and enjoy a successful career in League soccer, most notably with Sheffield Wednesday and Arsenal, after helping the Tigers to promotion from the old Fourth Division in 1982-83. But Billy had helped him with his grounding in the game and Roy Bly said: "In the early days I think Brian would accept how disciplined my dad made him. He would say: 'If you earn four quid, son, then one pound goes into the building society. Save a little.' That helped him on his way.

"And Brian would never dare to have an alcoholic drink in his hand in my dad's presence. Occasionally we'd see him in the players' lounge after a game at Boothferry Park and, when my dad came in, he'd shudder and pass his pint along the bar. He'd say to me: 'Don't tell your dad I've been drinking!'"

Billy Bly's links with Hull City and North Ferriby United, in fact, are still preserved today. Roy, who played for Ferriby in their Yorkshire League days - mainly as a right-back - from August 1971 for three years, explained: "When dad passed away, Roy Wallis, who was the secretary at the time, came to see me and said that they wanted to introduce some sort of trophy in his memory. A supporter, who wanted to remain anonymous, was making a trophy and they wanted to know in what way they could use it in an event for my father. I had a word with my mum and it was a natural decision really because of the connection between Hull City and the work that he used to do with North Ferriby.

"At one stage there was some talk about awarding it for a Goalkeeper of the Year, but to me it was better to play what has become an annual pre-season fixture between Hull City and North Ferriby for the Billy Bly Memorial Trophy. It's an unusual trophy because it's carved wood with a glass frame and top and a copper-made goalpost with a figurine of a goalkeeper making a save. At one time there was a key in the figure of a goalkeeper to open the top of the trophy."

The first Billy Bly Memorial Trophy game took place on July 29, 1985, and coincided with former England, Manchester United, West Ham United and Hull City striker Stuart Pearson opening Ferriby's new £12,000 dressing-rooms at Church Road. It was also the day on which the Tigers heard that an independent tribunal had fixed a £70,000 fee for their midfield player Steve McClaren, later to become one of the country's top coaches, to join Derby County, but they won 4-0 with goals by Billy Whitehurst (two), Frank Bunn and Garreth Roberts. Bunn and Neil Williams made their debuts for the Tigers that night, Pearson guested for Ferriby and Raich Carter fittingly presented the trophy to Roberts, the winning captain. Since then it has been presented to the winners by Roy Bly and Brian Marwood at various times, while Roy and his sister, Norma, still make a point of attending the game that keeps their famous father's name alive in East Riding soccer.

Sadly, Billy's own life ended when he was just 61. Even though he had always had pride in his approach to fitness, he had started to be dogged by ill-health in the early 1980s. Gradually matters got worse and Roy remembered: "Over the years we'd always go away to see relatives and that would be a holiday to my dad. When I was younger, he would take us up to Cullercoats, north of Newcastle near Whitley Bay, where my Auntie Winnie and Uncle Bob lived. We'd have a week there and then on another occasion we'd go down to Hughenden Manor, near Wycombe, where my Auntie Maud and Uncle Billy were. We'd also go down to Parkstone as well.

"In the summer of 1981 dad went up to Newcastle to collect my Auntie Winnie and then he drove down to see my Auntie Bella on my mum's side at Stevenage. While he was on his way there, he was dehydrating without realising it, so he drunk three bottles of lemonade on his journey. Subsequently his temperature went higher, so he was taken into hospital. He was in there for three weeks and then there was convalescence for a few months after that.

"He had smoked and he had a bronchial problem, so he was off work for some time. I remember going down to Stevenage to pick up his car, but he did manage to drive again eventually. We used to take him out to help him to recuperate because he'd had to spend a lot of time in bed. His muscles needed building up and he had to get used to walking again, so we had some family days out. He spent Christmas with us and seemed to be okay. In fact, he eventually went back to work on January 18, 1982, but I think that he was put on light duties.

"Then one day he wasn't feeling too well at work. That night he wasn't too well at all and unfortunately he collapsed the following morning. Basically his arteries closed up on him, so it looked as if he had had a massive heart attack. The coroner basically concluded that bronchial and artery problems had caused his death. He had been a reasonably heavy smoker - about 10 cigarettes a day - and undoubtedly it was contributory."

Billy Bly died at home on March 24, 1982, and there was a certain soccer poignancy to its timing because Roy pointed out: "On the weekend before he died, we went to watch Brian Marwood play for Hull City because they were at home to Port Vale. We went into the boardroom and Raich Carter was there. Dad hadn't seen him for a while and they had a really good chinwag about the old days. People recognised dad and he was allowed to park his car at the ground. It was still the old cinder track that he had trained on when he'd been a player - there was no supermarket at that time. After the game he came back to our house for a cup of tea and that was the last time that I saw him alive. On the Monday morning I got the call from my mum.

"I regret not having talked through a lot of things with him. I couldn't believe that my dad's death warranted a report on the front page of the Hull Daily Mail. We received cards and telephone calls. In that sense it was wonderful and I was very, very moved. Mum was absolutely shattered by it all, of course. There were a lot of people at the funeral and the Chanterlands Avenue Crematorium was packed out. Mum didn't want any music and it was a very sullen and sombre occasion.

"There were a lot of football people there and there was a busload from Everthorpe. But I was very disappointed with the vicar and I regret that we didn't ask the chaplain at Everthorpe to take the service. The guy stood there and literally told the congregation that playing football on a Sunday shouldn't really have been allowed and didn't make it any kind of celebration of my dad's life. It was a very poor service because I'm sure that someone else would have brought out a lot of warmth and happiness. There were a lot of good words that could have been said, but at least it was well-attended."

There was also a footballing pathos about the timing of Billy's death. He had scaled the heights with Hull City, playing in front of the highest attendances in the club's history. In those immediate postwar years the Needler family had given the public every hope that the club would become one of the biggest in the country. Billy had been one of the heroes who had been there when there had been genuine ambition, but his death came just a month after the Needler family had allowed everything to get out of hand financially to such a disastrous extent that the club had had to go embarrassingly into receivership.

Billy Bly's death brought the memories flooding back of an all-too-brief golden era at a time when City's stock was at its lowest to date. The comparison encapsulated the extremes of fortune that the public of East Yorkshire had had to endure with regard to professional soccer. As a result, Billy had even been mentioned whimsically and lovingly in the Guardian's leader column on February 26, 1982, just before his death: "We are not yet two months into it, but already 1982 looks like being the Year of the Receiver. Such things would have been unthinkable in the days when Raich Carter packed the crowds into Boothferry Park, when Don Revie thought it worthwhile to move there from Leicester City and when Alf Ackerman and Chris Chilton season by season whacked hatfuls of goals past the Second Division's astonished custodians. The football public should learn to think of the receiver simply as a form of financial goalkeeper, able to field all that comes at him and keep a clean scoresheet at the end - not so spectacular perhaps, but, deep down, no more than a pin-striped counterpart of the great Billy Bly."

There was also some consolation that Raich Carter was quick to pay tribute to Billy publicly: "I don't think City will ever have a finer 'keeper. There has been a lot of talk in recent years about the important part that goalkeepers play in the game and how good they have become. But, to my way of thinking, they have always been good in this country. I can remember such as Elisha Scott, Harry Hibbs, Frank Swift and Frank Moss and I rate Billy in that category. It was unfortunate that he was prone to injury, but he played a great part in preserving our defensive record while I was at Boothferry Park. He was consistent and never let us down. More than that, he was a very good chap off the field. He was amiable, good company and a joy to be with."

Billy Bly was cremated and his ashes were scattered in the local cemetery at Cottingham. His beloved Dorothy found it difficult to stay in their home in Thornwick Avenue, Willerby, and a few months after his death she moved a few avenues away to a bungalow in the Parkway, where Hull City had had a lot of club houses at one stage. She later moved to Pocklington for 10 years before finally returning to Willerby.

Just as Billy had been at Boothferry Park for a game shortly before his death in 1982, so was Dorothy. During the summer of 1996 she was poorly while taking a family holiday in Torquay and went for some tests on her return. But she and Roy were invited to Boothferry Park on August 31, 1996, as guests of the club for what turned out to be a goalless draw against Barnet. It was the 50th anniversary of another goalless draw - against Lincoln City - in which Billy had played and been injured in the first-ever game at Boothferry Park.

Maybe it provided some sort of symmetry and took the story full circle in various ways because Dorothy died in Hull Royal Infirmary a few months afterwards - on December 2, 1996. She was buried in Cottingham Cemetery - not far from the memorial stone that signifies Billy's ashes.

12

An All-Time Great

It is now 20 years since Billy Bly's death and the majority of today's Hull City supporters will have never seen him play and may know of him only as a vague name from the past. They may care just about the present and the future, but it is also imperative that the players who formed a major part of the club's heritage should be permitted and awarded the respect that they deserved. Some of those who passed through the Tigers' ranks and their achievements will live in the memories of those who were fortunate to have been able to watch them perform at their best. Some will go on a stage further in the public perception and earn themselves a classification as an all-time great.

It is an entirely a personal perception of what defines "an all-time great" and it is always essential that such a term should not be bandied about carelessly, injudiciously or excessively. But Billy Bly arguably merits the acronym in Hull City terms and there is overwhelming evidence that he enjoyed the utmost respect from colleagues and supporters alike.

Above all, the loyalty factor is always a trump card to be played when analysing Billy Bly's contribution to Hull City. Times have changed and modern players flit from club to club at the drop of a coin or two. It did not happen in Billy's day because the scope was not there: the maximum wage was instead. It is unthinkable nowadays that any player will emulate Billy's achievement of staying with one club for 23 years ever again. One simple statistics sums it up in Billy Bly's case: he was playing for Hull City before Barry Lord, who became one of his goalkeeping teammates at Boothferry Park, was born in November 1937.

Today footballers are looked-after well and rightly so. But they are pampered in comparison with some of the conditions that someone such as Billy had to endure in another era. The kit and equipment have improved out of all recognition since Billy's hey-day and he once reminisced about his fate: "The worst thing about wearing a thick goalkeeping jumper was that in the hot weather you'd sweat a lot. The roll-neck would chafe your skin and you'd get some bad rashes with it. Then in the wintertime the mud used to get into your jersey when you were diving around. I once played at Southampton and had my sleeves rolled up to my elbows. And even at halftime they were still hanging down and my jersey was hanging over the top of my shorts because it was stretching. I had to get a lace to fasten round the jersey and my shorts so that the jersey wouldn't go any farther. I didn't have a change of strip. I went out for the second half. And when I came off at the final whistle, I just took it off, but I dropped it. One of the lads picked it up and said: 'Bill, how have you been running around and jumping around with that on? It's a ton weight. I never felt anything like it in my life for playing football in!'

"And the old leather ball used to start off all right, but in bad weather the leather used to absorb the water and moisture. It used to get heavier and heavier and heavier as the game wore on. And by the time that the game was finishing, then I was doing well if I were able to kick it halfway between the penalty area and the halfway line."

Times have changed and it is almost impossible to comprehend the conditions and circumstances that prevailed in Billy's day. He played in an era when loyalty spoke volumes and footballers were, to all intents and purposes, on a par with the average working man. The only major difference was they were privileged enough and talented enough to mix business with pleasure and earn their livings from something that they passionately enjoyed - sport. They knew that they were fortunate, though, and accepted it graciously. Money, therefore, was not all-consuming.

Billy merely set his own standards as a player and a person. In fact, he was often immaculate - with the possible exception of his goalkeeping cap! His wife, Dorothy, insisted: "He was a lovely man and was one of the best-dressed players of the day. Wages were beginning to rise just as Billy left City. We would have been millionaires now because he was a real star. I have no regrets, though, because that's how life was and you didn't know any other. Billy enjoyed every minute of it. We were both very sad when he had to give up the game, but I suppose that all good things must come to an end. I'd love to live it all over again because the players enjoyed their football in those days."

Billy, of course, just put up with the adversity and got on with life because he was an easy-going character outwardly, but that hid a steely, single-minded determination. He tended to balk at controversy although there were bound to be some moments of dispute during such a long and distinguished career.

There was one, for example, in a match in January 1947 when the Tigers went behind before winning 4-2 at Accrington Stanley. Ex-Tiger Dennis Smith was ruled to have opened the scoring for Stanley in the 19th minute with a lob which Bly "flicked against the under portion of the crossbar, catching and clearing on the rebound." The referee signalled a goal because he felt that the ball had crossed the line and City's players surged round him. He was forced to consult his linesman - regrettably not a Russian one - and stood by his decision. Bly may well have been annoyed inwardly, but in life in general his reaction was to be philosophical on the outside.

And recounting the story of someone who was a hero, idolised by the fans and in this instance considered by his public to be an all-time great tends to be one-dimensional even if it is true. Billy did make errors: there is always the human element to take into account. In terms of goalkeepers, their reputations are built or destroyed on the basis of consistency. They all make some mistakes, but those who make the fewest last the longest. And they remain a breed apart because they have the added pressure of usually being the last line of defence and their blunders are usually costly and mean the concession of a goal.

Billy did occasionally drop clangers and there are tales that at times he would blame anyone but himself for conceding a goal. It is perfectly understandable in one sense because goalkeepers live in a world in which they have to believe that the only way in which they are blameless and unimpeachable is if they keep clean sheets.

They are a special type at the best of times simply because they have a special type of challenge game in and game out. They can often be outstanding, for example, and still end up on the losing side. After all, they demonstrate their skills only when their 10 outfield comrades on the field have in effect left them to it. Normally goalkeepers are described as mad simply because they have become goalkeepers in the first place.

Winger Mike Bowering, for example, remembered a 3-1 home win over Brentford when he and Billy were teammates during the 1958-59 promotion season in the old Third Division. Billy was beaten by a speculative shot by Brentford's winger Dennis Heath for a soft goal in only the second minute and his public explanation was that the ball had skidded, knocked back one of his fingers and then hit his legs before going in. But Bowering said: "Billy let the ball go through his hands and then said at halftime that he had had a blind spot because of the floodlights! Bob Brocklebank then doubted that the lights had even come on so early in the game!" Typically, though, Billy put the incident behind him as he showed that necessary mental toughness that all goalkeepers need and it was reported: "Bly did not allow his early slip to upset him as he made a number of good saves."

On another occasion he was in trouble when he did not get back to the team coach in time after a match. Teammate Denis Durham recalled: "We played at Hartlepool and Bill had some relatives come down from Newcastle to see the game. He went to see them straight after it and he hadn't turned up at the coach when it was time to go, so the manager, Major Frank Buckley, just said that it was Bill's hard luck because he should have been there."

Billy's indiscretions, though, were rare and the biggest setbacks in his football career were accidental because they surrounded his injury lay-offs. Daily Sketch journalist Laurie Pignon once wrote that he had "suffered enough injuries to keep Emergency Ward 10 going." And it is interesting to estimate how many appearances he would have made for the Tigers if the injuries had not been the bane of his life. Andy Davidson, another loyal City servant, leads the way overall with a record of 520 in the League for the club. He, too, suffered serious injuries at times, but how many more appearances would Billy have made than his 403 if he had not been forced on to the sidelines so often?

The injuries brought a sense of pathos to his career, especially when he was hurt in the friendly against Falkirk in 1954 and had to miss his call-up for the England B party. Even though he had played with and against some of the best, he had instead to be content with representative honours for the Third Division North against the Third Division South. They tended to be the representative games that football forgot and his appearance with his City teammate Johnny Stephens for the Third Division North at Carlisle United's Brunton Park in March 1958 was in doubt at one stage because there was controversy about the date and the venue.

But Billy did not miss out even though it meant that he had to play three games in four days. The match took place on March 18, but the previous evening City had been at home to Tranmere Rovers and two days earlier they had drawn 1-1 at Chester. There again Billy played three League games in four days the following month because that was how the Easter holiday programme was planned in those days. The Tigers, in fact, fitted 15 League games into March and April in 1958 - almost a third of their programme. But the concept of burn-out was never mentioned, the players never moaned and they just went out and played for the sheer enjoyment of it all.

There were other instances of anti-climax that must have made Billy wonder what he had done to deserve such ill-fortune. When he played in the City team of 1948-49 who began the season with a record-breaking run of nine successive League victories, the Football League rejected a request from the club to present the players with mementoes of their achievement. In addition, Billy never had the opportunity to test himself in the top flight of English League soccer and Roy Bly observed: "He never came out with it outright and said that he was disappointed about not having played in the First Division, but I'm sure he did think about it."

Outwardly, though, Billy Bly always got on with life and shrugged off the disappointments. But his patience and behaviour were tested to the full by the manner of his departure from Hull City after 23 years' service because it was totally unsatisfactory and shameful on the club's part. It led to a major public outcry and there is little doubt that it hurt Billy deep inside, but he largely kept his thoughts to himself because he was not one for making a fuss and the fans' virulent and vitriolic protests probably embarrassed him even though he was doubtless grateful for their loyal support at a time of disloyalty from the club.

He was essentially phlegmatic, but at the same time he would not be pushed about if he thought that there were a principle at stake, as he demonstrated when he had the confrontation with new trainer Angus McLean as to which way he should run round Boothferry Park's perimeter in training. His teammates openly admit that they found the scenario immensely amusing, but Billy felt that he was making a salient point about maintaining a routine that had held him in good stead.

At the same time he rarely let his emotions get the better of him. He had his strong beliefs and thoughts and sometimes he expressed them, but he was not the kind of person to create a hullabaloo. He normally preferred to keep his innermost feelings in check instead and top playwright Alan Plater once said of him, possibly with a hint of a pun in view of his stint as a shopkeeper: "Billy was a sweet man and a superb 'keeper, who fractured easily."

Billy earned the respect of his colleagues and his public and also gained respect from his opponents. He, in turn, appreciated them and tried to find ways of dealing with the most difficult of them. Billy regarded Welsh international hero John Charles as his toughest opponent. He once claimed that Charles and former Northern Ireland star Danny Blanchflower were the only players to have hit shots so hard that he never saw them. In addition, he was respectful of the heading prowess of both Charles and former England centre-forward Tommy Lawton because he said: "They are often reported as flicking the ball with their heads, but they place it with incredible accuracy. I always punch clear and never attempt to catch the ball with either of them around."

Respect for Billy, though, came his way in different guises. He is basically remembered as somebody with a kind heart and talented hands. Those hands came to Hull City's rescue for 23 years, but they were handy in other ways because of his artistic flair, his carpentry and his cobbling. And a classic example occurred when inmates at Everthorpe Borstal asked him to draw sketches for them of Elvis Presley, the king of rock-and-roll who died in 1977 while Billy was working there.

On another equally-memorable occasion Billy's ability to make friends and gain admirers wherever he went meant that he was even praised in a church sermon. It happened when City's player-manager Raich Carter and his players attended a service at St. Mary's Church, Beverley. Their appearance attracted a congregation of about 1,000 people - the biggest gathering at the church for many years - with hundreds of others left outside. Carter read the lessons and Canon Thomas Tardrew talked about footballers' courage during his sermon. He referred specifically to Bly's broken nose in the Tigers' FA Cup defeat by Manchester United in 1949, adding: "I wish that more of our people had the moral courage of which the physical courage of Billy Bly is a counterpart. We can learn many lessons from the endurance and courage of the footballer."

While Billy achieved success with his hands, his feet remained firmly on the ground. He showed touches of humility, for example, when he regularly collected autographs of his colleagues for himself. He garnered the signatures of his teammates during the War when they were photographed and he had a penchant for having dinner menus signed. He did not play, for example, in the end-of-season East Riding Invitation Trophy game against Grimsby Town in late May 1947 when City won 1-0 with a goal by Denis Thompson. Peter Atkinson was in goal, but Billy attended the accompanying dinner at Hull Guildhall afterwards and collected autographs of players from both sides on the back of the menu. The following season, in fact, City held their own dinner at Hull's Royal Station Hotel on March 14, 1950, and Billy again obtained all the autographs of his teammates on the menu.

Billy always maintained more than a modicum of modesty and that might well have been attributed to his strong family background from childhood to adulthood. He thought the world of his family and they thought the world of him. He was always there for his family even if his advice did not pay dividends all the time because his nephew Chris Mawson wrily observed: "Uncle Billy did try to teach me how to play football, but the Bly magic did not get passed to this side of the family!"

Billy's colleagues also emphasise his kindness when they evaluate him as a person. They repeatedly refer to his help and counsel, which were always on tap for those who wanted to listen. He was generous and giving and time and again he proved that there really was no edge to him.

Jimmy Greenhalgh, who played alongside Billy in the first game at Boothferry Park in 1946 after joining the Tigers from non-League football in Lancashire and missed only one match during their successful 1948-49 campaign, recalled: "It gives me great pleasure to think about Billy Bly and those times at Hull City, where I started my career in League football. Our manager then was Major Frank Buckley, who was famous in the game for his ability to develop young players into quality ones. Bill was then not only a senior, but one of the best 'keepers in the League and a great teacher to players such as myself who were just coming into the game as professional footballers.

"I feel so grateful for having the honour and luck to have started my football career with the help and guidance of Bill and his colleagues. They were not only teammates, but also teachers of the game, of life and of the high standards required from the players in regard to our supporters and fans.

"My best memories are from Hull City and the players such as Bill who showed me what the game and the business were all about. They taught me so much about football that my career in it carried on until I reached the age of 60. I was lucky to have known Bill, who was a legend in the game."

The same basic sentiments were echoed by Johnny Neal, who, like Greenhalgh, had a spell as a manager in the North-East where football passions are so strong. Neal reflected: "When I think of what my greatest team ever would be, there would always be either Billy Bly or Nigel Sims from Aston Villa in goal.

"I was only a youngster when I was out there at Hull City playing in front of one of the largest supporter bases there was. I was asking players such as Billy what to do, but they carried me. The older professionals brought on the younger ones and instilled discipline. It gave me great experience, but that's what used to happen and, thanks to people such as Billy, it helped me for the years ahead."

Neal also mused about the manner of his own departure from Boothferry Park in comparison with the treatment handed out to Bly. It taught him a lesson and it stayed with him when he later branched out into management: "I didn't stay long at Hull City under Bob Brocklebank and the only way as a player that you get away from a League club in those days was to go into non-League, so I went to King's Lynn because the manager, Paul Todd, was an ex-Hull player. Eventually Bert Head moved in for me and took me to Swindon Town and before long I went on to Aston Villa and finally Southend United.

"But things were done differently in those early days and, as Billy found out, often they were handled in a cruel and crude way. That was the way it was, but I promised myself that, if I ever handled people in management, then it would be in a proper way because you get back what you put in. But the principles of the players and characters I was with at Hull City have stayed with me to this day."

Billy then was much more than just a teammate. He was someone to be respected and admired, he was a friend and adviser, he was available, accessible and approachable and he was a teacher and mentor who readily and freely passed on the fruits of his experience.

Brian Bulless said: "On leaving school, I signed amateur forms for Hull City and started playing for the juniors. Training was on Tuesday and Thursday nights at Boothferry Park and one night Bill came in to have some extra treatment on an arm injury. Jimmy Lodge was the club's medical man and he introduced me to Bill. From that night we became big friends and he was always available for any help or advice if I or anyone else wanted it. We shared some good times together, he had a long and wonderful career with Hull City and I felt privileged to have played in the same team with him."

Colin Smith reflected: "Billy was the goalkeeping hero who dived at opposing players' feet, made great saves and suffered many injuries. After settling in at Hull City, I got to know Billy simply because he was the one senior player who went out of his way to make me feel at home. The occasional: 'Hello, son, how's it going?' was very welcome. Bill was one of the nicest people I had the good fortune to call a mate and it was a sad day when he died in his early 60s."

Mike Brown recalled: "Billy was very, very pleasant and always had a smile on his face. He was not toffee-nosed in any way and I'd loved to have known him better and played more games in front of him."

Charlie Crickmore added: "I had a great deal of respect for Billy Bly. He was a grand character. He was near the end of his career when I was just beginning mine with people such as Joe Stocks, Chris Morris, Roger Cowling and Chris Chilton, but I found him such a gentleman and a brilliant guy. If you had any problems from a coaching point of view, he liked to talk and Billy Bly, Andy Davidson and Brian Bulless were like big brothers to me."

Billy's fellow goalkeepers were effectively his adversaries for one berth in the side as well as teammates, but his co-operation naturally extended to them as well. Len Round recalled: "Billy was more experienced than I was, but he never minded helping me at all. He was some goalie." And Bernard Fisher added: "My memories of Billy are of the most conscientious, hard-working footballer I met. He was friendly, helpful, caring, brave and at times mad, like all 'keepers. We never had a cross word although we were rivals in goal and he helped me more than I could return the compliment."

Other teammates remembered him as a genuine nice guy whose goalkeeping abilities should have earned him greater recognition and appreciation. Jack Bennion said: "He was a fine man and just a good goalkeeper. He was one of the best uncapped goalkeepers around in his day. He had many, many good games and very few bad ones because he was a very consistent goalkeeper. He'd still be up there with the best I've seen - even today." And Mike Bowering added: "He was a gentleman and one of the nicest people you could ever hope to meet. He was also a very good goalkeeper and he'd have been capped by England if he'd have played for another club."

Billy's down-to-earth, disarming modesty about his achievements also endeared him to those who knew him from Hull City to North Ferriby United. Norman Moore played alongside him during the early years of Boothferry Park: "Billy was a smashing lad and was always friendly towards people. He was a good sportsman and, if he made a good save and we congratulated him, he'd say that he was just doing his job." Mike Rawding worked with him much later in management at North Ferriby: "Quite often someone would mention on our away trips to the home supporters who Billy was if he had not already been recognised and they would want to talk about various games or ask for his autograph. No-one was ever refused. And if ever any of them praised his performance in a particular game that they'd seen, he would usually pass it off with: 'Yes, I was lucky that day.'"

Billy Bly then is remembered by his contemporaries on two levels and Denis Durham put it into perspective when he said: "I was full of respect for him both as a goalkeeper and as a person." And Brian Cripsey, who emigrated to New Zealand, added: "He was a great guy and a wonderful goalkeeper." Doug Clarke lyrically lauded him: "Billy was extremely loyal to his club and teammates. When Billy was released, I found it shoddy and demeaning for such a servant to Hull City to be treated in the way that he was. Billy was a Tiger through and through and deserved better. In my fading career memories his face still shines brightly and clearly as a true teammate and top man."

It all served to make Billy Bly someone special who would never be forgotten in the annals of Hull City. Dave Fraser, who was a colleague at both City and Everthorpe Borstal, said: "At one time he was the third most important person in Hull - there was the Lord Mayor, Raich Carter and Billy Bly. And if you ask who were the greatest footballers to play for Hull City, then people such as Neil Franklin and Raich Carter come first because they were truly international-class. But if you want an honest opinion as to the most popular player ever with fans, then it is Billy Bly without any shadow of doubt." And City's record appearances holder Andy Davidson, who served them for 31 years because he stayed on in management after retiring as a player, added: "As I got to know Billy through the years, I learned to appreciate what a goalkeeper he was. In my humble opinion he was the best 'keeper I played with or against. I don't think I will ever see another Billy Bly."

Billy had his own perspective because he said in an interview in March 1955: "Sometimes I have been called 'the India Rubber Man' because of my acrobatic style of keeping. But there have been many occasions when I wished my bones were a lot more pliable. Then perhaps I would not have got so many breaks. But don't think I am complaining. Although unfortunate to miss a fair number of matches through injury, I have always had the incredible luck to get back to a first-team place with Hull City. Some years ago my mother asked me to give up playing when my injury run was at its worst. For a time I considered her plea, but eventually decided I could not leave the game I love so much. And if I had my life over again, I would go through it all again - for football."

It underlined his great gratitude for the chance to be able to do something that he loved and to be paid for doing so. It is sadly an attitude from yesteryear and it is a basic approach that made him so universally popular as a goalkeeper and a person. Billy Bly summed it all up ever so neatly on another occasion when he mused: "I would not change my lot for anyone in the game. I have enjoyed every minute. I love the game. Nobody twisted my arm to make me play." Needless to say, the India Rubber Man would have surely broken it if anyone had done so...